Once Upon the Lagan

On the River Lagan, Belfast.

Once Upon the Lagan

The Story of the Lagan Canal

·MAY BLAIR

THE
BLACKSTAFF
PRESS

BELFAST

First published in June 1981 by
The Blackstaff Press Limited
Blackstaff House, Wildflower Way, Apollo Road
Belfast BT12 6TA, Northern Ireland

Reprinted December 1981, with corrections; 1983;
1994 with corrections; 2000

Printed in Ireland by ColourBooks Limited

A CIP catalogue record for this book
is available from the British Library

ISBN 0-85640-245-1

www.blackstaffpress.com

CONTENTS

PREFACE
TO THE FIFTH IMPRESSION

People have often asked me why I wrote this book. I tell them that in a world of rapid change I wanted to record a particular way of life – the life of the lock-keeper, the hauler, the lighterman, the bank-ranger – before the last of that generation was dead and gone. And in the nineteen years that have elapsed since *Once Upon the Lagan* was first published, the canal folk, whose memories fill these pages, have indeed passed away. However, thanks to the initiative and enthusiasm of a number of individuals and public agencies, their memories may now come to life again.

A management strategy for the Lagan Valley was commissioned by the Environment and Heritage Service and implemented in booklet form in 1996. It contains much food for thought. Will the dream ever become a reality? The signs are good.

Lisburn Borough Council's vision for the future includes the development of the Lagan Valley Regional Park, parallel with the revitalisation of the river for recreational and commercial use, and thanks to that body, the Island Mill site is an island again with the excavation of the old lock and adjoining stretch of canal. Two new access bridges have been added and a brand-new civic centre occupies the island itself.

Downstream at Seymour Hill another bridge has been constructed for the convenience of ramblers using the tow-path. And at Newforge a feasibility study is being carried out by Castlereagh Borough Council on the possibility of restoring the lock and lockhouse to their former glory for use as an educational and interpretive centre. But the most breathtaking changes have taken place in the lower reaches of the river below Stranmillis (thanks to the initiative of Laganside Corporation) where we have the Waterfront Hall and the Hilton Hotel on the site of the old May's Market. I wonder what the canal folk would make of it all!

MAY BLAIR
MAZE, JUNE 2000

ACKNOWLEDGEMENTS

A book of this nature cannot be produced without the help of very many people. I cannot name everybody who contributed during the several years it took to complete the research, but I am deeply indebted to all who did. I will never forget the courtesy extended to me by the many people to whom I was a stranger, and who perhaps found my insistent questions somewhat annoying and my all-absorbing interest in an almost forgotten canal unusual, if not downright odd.

As well as the canal folk, among whom stand out the names of Joe McVeigh, George Weir, James Hanna, Rosaleen Mulholland, Susan Agnew and Paddy Creaney, I must also name individually those people who went out of their way to give me additional extensive information and advice, and leads which proved most helpful. Among them were Hugh McIlgorm, Robert Emerson, Eliza Lilley and the brothers James, Thomas and John Taggart; also Will Best, who not only helped, but 'went the second mile' and wrote the script and provided the pictures for Chapter V and Cecil Kilpatrick for information drawn from his Kilpatrick family tree.

I must also thank Elsie Greer and the people of St James' Primary School for it was in St James' that the seeds of this interesting study were sown.

Thanks are due also to the staffs of Ballynahinch and Belfast Public Libraries, the Linen Hall Library, the Lisburn Museum, the Public Record Office of Northern Ireland, the Ulster Folk and Transport Museum, and Rathvarna Teachers' Centre, Lisburn.

In particular, I would like to thank Bill Crawford who not only read the script and advised accordingly, but also gave encouragement when it was most needed.

Acknowledgement must also be made to those who typed the script, Margaret Megarry and Rita Thompson who did some of it, and Salome Adams who did most of it and who was always able to rise to the occasion when a deadline was given.

Last but by no means least I must thank those who gave permission to reproduce the many photographs which enhance this book and without which it might never have been written: the Public Record Office of Northern Ireland (pp. 13, 42); the Ulster Folk and Transport Museum (pp. 26, 94, 101); the National Library of Ireland (p. 27); the *Belfast Telegraph* (pp. 31, 73); the *Belfast Newsletter* (pp. 49, 53, 78) and the Ministry of Finance Works Division (p. 77), all per Dr W.A. McCutcheon; Dr E.M. Patterson (pp. 43, 46,

47). The aerial photograph on p. 24 was taken by Aero Pictorial Ltd., London, and supplied by Daniel McWilliam.

The picture of the lighter at Shaw's Bridge on p. 10 and the painting 'Barges at Edenderry' by Romeo Toogood are from the Ulster Museum Collection; 'Trees on the Lagan' by William Conor is from the Ulster Folk and Transport Museum; 'Snow on the Lagan' by Conor is from a private collection.

For the photographs on pp. 2, 6, 14, 15, 16, 18, 20, 54, 76 and 127, originally commissioned by the Lambeg Bleaching Dyeing and Finishing Company for use as evidence against the Navigation Company in the House of Lords, I am indebted to Thomas Muir.

Abner Peel, John Foy and Stanley Burns (who also took the beautiful photographs on pp. 17, 34, 40, 41, 57, 67, 72, 86 and 124) are all to be thanked for their work in so ably copying the old documents and photographs for me.

In addition I must thank the following individuals who supplied photographs from their own private collections: George Weir, Maureen Boswell, Robert McCurley, Ken Kelly, Stanley Kilpatrick, Tom McDevitte, W.A. Thompson, W.J. McCartney, Daniel McWilliam, James Hanna, H. Beaumont, Frederick W. Browne, Nora Stronge, Molly Kelsey, Estlin Agnew, T. Reynolds, Joe McVeigh, Harry McCourt, Rosaleen Mulholland, Elizabeth Hanna, Thomas Taggart, Edward Lavery, Ernest Kennedy, Emma Gregg, Andrew Murray, Elizabeth Stewart, Hugh McIlgorm, D. McMeekin, Joan Emerson and Betty Acheson.

I am also grateful to the many others who wrote, telephoned or submitted photographs which we were unable to include; their interest and encouragement meant so much to me.

I hope the end product is a verbal and pictorial record worthy of the world of local history and that it may prove of permanent value for reference, refresh old memories of bygone days and encourage those perusing its pages to go and do likewise.

Yours in research,
May Blair

LIST OF ILLUSTRATIONS

I
'DOWN THE LINE'
FROM
MOLLY WARD'S

Oh Molly Ward's, you're silent now
Compared to days that have gone by,
When lighters lay there in a row
To wait the day when they must go.
No engine then to drive them through,
Just line, and horse, and hauler too.

Thus wrote hauler Harry O'Rawe, who worked on the Lagan Canal in the years following the 1914–18 World War. Today you might have difficulty in finding Molly Ward's lock on a map, but this now derelict spot at Stranmillis was once a vital valve in the transport system of Northern Ireland. Thousands of tons **of merchandise** were imported annually through Belfast and transported from Molly Ward's by horse-drawn barge, or 'lighter', to destinations as distant as Monaghan, Coalisland and Portglenone. The path of the canal lay in the Lagan Valley as far as Lisburn (indeed most of it lay in the river itself), but from Lisburn to Moira its path lay directly underneath the present motorway. The whins which delight the eye along this stretch of roadway in early summer are the same whins that flanked canal on one side and well-trodden towpath on the other, as ponderous horse and cumbersome barge once made their leisurely way towards Ellis' Gut in the south-east corner of Lough Neagh.

There were twenty-seven locks on the Canal, with eighteen lock-keepers to look after them. The lock-keeper's main duty was to pass all lighters and other craft through the locks in their proper order – which was sometimes difficult, as there was the occasional argument as to which lighterman had reached the lock first. Each lighterman had to be issued with an official permit, and at some locks the measurement of draught had to be checked and entered on the permit. (A change in draught would have indicated that the cargo had been tampered with, or that the lighter was leaking.) The lock-keeper had also to avoid any

'Barges at Edenderry' by Romeo Toogood
(Collection: Ulster Museum, Belfast).

1

No. 3 lock filled with water, ready for a boat
coming downstream (1924).

LAGAN NAVIGATION COMPANY.

REGULATIONS

FOR

LOCK-KEEPERS

No. 1—No Lock-Keeper shall absent himself from his duties, or entrust these to any deputy, without the authority of the Inspector, on pain of dismissal, or of such fine as the Directors may inflict.

No. 2—The Lock-Keeper shall carefully watch over the Banks, Towing-paths, Locks, Weirs, Overflows, Waste Sluices, Bridges, and Quays, and keep in repair the Banks and Roads under his charge, and shall report without delay, to the Inspector, anything in the state of the works that requires immediate attention, under a penalty of 10s.

No. 3—The Lock-Keeper shall require the production of the Permit before passing any Boat or Lighter through his Locks, and shall enter the same in his book, under a penalty of 2s. 6d.

No. 4—The Lock-Keeper shall not permit the discharge of any cargo, or portion thereof, from a Lighter, while in the Chamber of the Locks; he shall not allow Lighter Masters or others to use Boat-hooks or Spiked Poles, in pushing Lighters out on the Lock Chamber; nor allow stones, or other materials, to be deposited on the banks or quays nearer to the water than 12 feet, nor allow the same to remain on banks or quays longer than 24 hours, under a penalty of 5s. for each offence.

No. 5—The Lock-Keepers shall attend to all Lighters that come at proper hours, but shall not pass any Lighters through the Locks at night, without an order in writing, from the Secretary or the Inspector, under a penalty of 5s.

No. 6—The Lock-Keeper shall keep his Short Gates locked after dark, and shall not allow any stranger to have access to, or the use of, handles, bars, or other implements for opening Locks, Pen Weirs, or Waste Sluices, under a penalty of £1.

No. 7—The Lock-Keeper shall not permit any Lighters to be moored within 60 yards of the Lock Gates, nor to enter the Locks unless there is sufficient water to carry them through the next level; nor, when Lighters pass allow the gates to close of themselves, under a penalty of 2s. 6d. for each offence.

No. 8—The Lock-Keeper shall not allow the Chamber of his Lock to remain full for half an hour at a time; nor, by carelessness or waste of water, suffer the level to be run so low as to obstruct the traffic, under a penalty of 5s.

No. 9—All Lock-Keepers, during dry weather, shall keep their gates properly secured with Moss, to prevent waste of water; and, when two or more Lighters are together, he shall pass them in each other's lock of water, under a penalty of 2s. 6d.

No. 10—The Lock-Keepers at Union Locks and Western levels on the Lagan Canal, and at Benburb and all other short reaches on the Ulster and Coalisland Canals, shall not run more water into the Chamber of the Lock than is necessary according to the fixed Gauge, to pass the Lighter, under a penalty of 10s.

No. 11—When a loaded Lighter enters a lock, the Lock-Keeper shall sound his horn, so as to give warning to all approaching Lighters, under a penalty of 10s.

No. 12—The Lock-Keeper shall not suffer the Racks to fall without winding them down, under a penalty of 5s.

No. 13—The Lock-Keepers at the entrance and outlet of each Canal shall not permit any Lighter to proceed at a greater draft of water than that allowed at the time, under a penalty of 10s.

(By order of the Directors,)

HENRY T. REA

The Lagan Navigation Company's 'Regulations for Lock-keepers'.

wastage of water when levels were low and prevent the lock from overflowing the banks in time of flood. In addition he (or she) had to keep the lock-basin clean and free from weeds and if necessary cut the weeds on the canal banks. Generally the lock-keeper was expected to do everything possible to preserve the rights of his employers, the Lagan Navigation Company, and maintain their property in good order. A copy of the Company's rules and regulations (left) had to be displayed at each lock.

Most of the eighteen lock-keepers had only one lock to attend to, though No. 14 had four (the 'Union Locks') and Nos. 15, 16 and 17 each had three. Seven of the lock-keepers in the lower section of the canal (Nos. 1, 2, 3, 6, 9, 11 and 12) also had weirs to look after. Their locks were situated in the artificial cuts by-passing bends in the river, where the water had to be maintained at a suitable level, usually by means of wooden pen-weirs. Weir-keeping required constant vigilance, day and night, during times of flood. This would have been impossible but for the fact that during floods boats could not sail, so there was no lock-keeping to do.

Each lock-keeper had a house and garden, except No. 12, who received an extra two shillings weekly in lieu of a garden. Several received a weekly cycling allowance of two shillings and sixpence in addition to their few pounds wages.

The Company's regulations set out that 'occupation of the lock-house was dependent upon employment with the company, and possession was to be given up "peaceably" upon termination of employment'.

The Company's income was derived from tolls, tug receipts, rents and transfer fees. Formerly most of this was collected by the lock-keeper at either end of the canal, either at Molly Ward's lock (Stranmillis) or in the case of downstream traffic at Ellis' Gut. The tolls were charged on the cargo at rates per ton varying with the distance travelled. The lock-keeper entered the tonnage and type of cargo on the permit, which also gave the date, name of lighter, lighterman's name, destination, amount paid, draft of lighter and the name of the owner. By far the busiest lock on the twenty-seven-mile length of canal was the first one, Molly Ward's, now a neglected and sorry sight.

Few people who look at the stagnant condition of this lock at Stranmillis to-day ever give a thought to the busy thriving place it once was. Some perhaps will remember the beautiful old Boat Club-house

A boat lies at anchor near Molly Ward's lock-
house *c*.1900.

with its slipway down to the canal, but only a few will recall the little thatched and whitewashed cottages (replaced by slated ones in 1913) which were once the cosy homes of Dick McCann and Dick McClelland – lock-keeper and bank-ranger on this once-busy part of the Lagan water. Other lock-keepers here included Robert T. Campbell, William Grattan, Tom Dooley, Richard Belshaw and, of course, Molly and William Ward; Jack Jones succeeded Dick McClelland as bank-ranger.

Molly Ward's was one of the seven locks where the lock-keeper had a pen-weir to attend to in addition to his lock. He also had to issue a permit stating the name of the boat, the draught, destination etc and, last but by no means least, he collected the tolls for the Navigation Company.

The premises of Belfast Boat Club now occupy the site where whitewash and thatch once made a scene fit for an artist's pallette. Where the hearth fire of Molly Ward's tavern once glowed, there now stands a modern tennis court; and where lighters lay in a row, there is today a landscaped amenity area and car park.

How different was the scene half a century ago when Cahal O'Byrne wrote:

It was the fairest summer weather. A sweet, strong wind from the south was blowing over the river meadows, where the browzing cattle stood knee-deep among the long lush fragrant grasses. The bright summer sunshine streamed over all the Lagan Valley and lay broad and golden on the river, darkened here and there by the green shadows that lay lazily sleeping under the drooping greenery by the waterside. The upland fields were rippling from shine to shade with the gold of their ripening corn. The green willow shadows and the green water met and blended where the sun-dazzle made lovelier all the waving green waterway. All was still, save where a rush of seething waters passed over the weir and wove in their passing a breadth of silver tissue fine as spider's spinning. In all this northern land there is no lovelier place for a summer ramble than round by the Lagan water up at Molly Ward's.

As I Roved Out, 2nd ed., 1970

Lightermen and haulers at the lock-keeper's
hut at Molly Ward's (No. 1 lock) in 1924.

Robert and Elizabeth McCurley by their lock-house at No. 2 in 1918. The lock – about ¼ ml downstream from the house – was called after Robert's uncle, Mickey Taylor.

Two hundred years ago, the hospitality of Molly Ward's tavern was well-known throughout the length and breadth of Ulster. Fashionable people of the day came from all airts and parts to sit in her river gardens and to partake not only of her ales and spirits, but also of her delectable 'cruds and cream'.

But there were more covert goings-on too. Molly Ward's was a favourite meeting place for the United Irishmen and regular visitors to her home included Wolfe Tone and Henry Joy McCracken. Arms were smuggled into Belfast Lough, and ferried in small pleasure-boats up to her tavern where they were stored prior to being distributed throughout the country, mostly to County Down. On one occasion, when it was feared that a raid by the military was imminent, a quantity of ammunition, guns and pike-heads was dumped in the nearby weir-hole. Just as the dreaded knock came to the door, it was discovered that a crock of powder had been overlooked. With great presence of mind and in true Irish fashion, Molly placed the crock by the fire, threw some clothes on top, and hastily invited her ageing mother-in-law to sit on it. She then placed her sleeping grandchild on the old woman's knee. While soldiers made a thorough search, Molly kept up a continuous prattle, even telling them where to find the antiquated weapon kept by her husband for the protection of the weir. The crock, of course, was never discovered.

But what of more recent times? Some of the older people in the district remember twenty, thirty or forty horses lined up early in the morning, patiently waiting for the loaded boats to arrive on the tide. Most of them were laden with coal, much of it destined for the Lagan Valley mills. If there was no flood, the lighter hooked on and moved off right away, but in time of flood there could be a delay of a day, a week or even several weeks. Not only would it have been dangerous to proceed, but often the flow of water was so strong that it would have been impossible for the horse to pull against it, even with the help of a second horse.

The second and third locks, like the first, were each situated at a point where a length of canal cut off a bend in the river. The island created between the river bend and the canal at the second lock was officially called Moreland's Meadow, but to the canal folk the spot was known as Mickey Taylor's. The name of Taylor is recorded at this lock in the years between 1860 and 1897. Later lock-keepers included Bob McCurley and John Rowan. In John's time improved road surfaces

Gibson's Bight – a passing place below the
third lock.

George Kilpatrick, lock-keeper at Newforge, lifts the handle of the sluice to let the water out of the lock.

and better drainage may have benefited the surrounding countryside but it created a real problem for him because of the increased volume and speed of drainage water entering the canal. As a result, lock-gates were often damaged or banks swept away by flood-water. In the spring of 1937 the flooding was so bad that the Rowan family were isolated for five days in their island-placed home. At one stage the water was three feet deep in their kitchen.

A wide curve leads to the third lock, Newforge (also known as McLeave's), where if you are lucky you might see a kingfisher skimming over the surface of the water. Here the towpath crosses over for the first time by means of a quaint blackstone bridge which is reminiscent of that depicted on a willow-pattern plate. The lock-house, situated close by, was occupied by James McLeave in the 1860s and 1870s. The last lock-keeper was George Kilpatrick, who arrived there in 1922 and stayed until his death in 1968. The Kilpatrick family tradition of working on the canal was similar to that of many canal folk. George was born in 1891, the sixth of the seven children of Alexander Kilpatrick (1849–1941). Alexander was a lock-keeper as was his twin brother Johnny (1849–1922). The brothers married sisters Anne and Liza Lynch whose brother George became manager of the canal in 1909. All three of Alexander's sons (James, Johnny and George) also became lock-keepers. When George started work at the age of fourteen, his first job was that of driving a horse and trap for Charlie Magowan, the then manager of the canal. Later he worked with the repair squad and eventually he also became a lock-keeper. He and his wife Sara reared ten children by the side of the Lagan and their youngest son Stanley still lives in the lock-house. Like most lock-keepers, George kept four or five goats, useful not only for their milk but also for cropping the grass at the sides of the towpath.

Continuing upstream from McLeave's lock, and passing Newforge, Shaw's Bridge is soon reached. This bridge took its name from a Captain Shaw who built an oak bridge there in 1655 to transport the guns of Cromwell's army across the river. In 1698 the wooden bridge was replaced by a stone one, but this was swept away by floods eleven years later. Another bridge was built in 1709 from the stones of the demolished Castle Carn. In 1976 a concrete bridge was opened close by because the old bridge was too narrow and becoming unsafe for heavy traffic. Shaw's Bridge was one of several where the towpath not only did not pass under the arches but also changed to the opposite side

A lighter passes under Shaw's Bridge near
Newforge.

Looking towards Newforge through an arch
of Shaw's Bridge.

of the river. A barge travelling up or downstream had to be unhitched,
the horse walked over the bridge, and the barge re-hitched on the
other side. This presented no problem as the horse soon learned to do
what was expected of him.

Just above Shaw's Bridge on the long level, Wilger's Well marked
the place where a young swimmer had been murdered. A little further
upstream a wide place on the river was known to lightermen as the
Washerwoman's Bight. The only visible shelter there was a hole in the

Shaw's Bridge, 1905. Horse and hauler pause for a moment as they cross over the bridge. To the right can be seen the mill race which drove the machinery for Harpur's clog factory.

The lighter *Industry* delivering coal from the Antrim Iron Ore Company to John Shaw Brown & Sons at Edenderry.

bank where the soil had come away, or had been scooped away from the roots of a huge beech. Incredibly this was the place of abode of an old crone by the name of Kate. Kate was a washerwoman, and a line of washing strung along the fence separating Barnett's Demesne from the towpath was at one time a familiar sight. On the opposite side, flanked by the Minnowburn beeches, is the Purdysburn, the first important tributary to enter the Lagan.

There were two locks on the three-mile stretch from Shaw's Bridge to Drumbridge (Nos. 4 and 5). The first was at Edenderry, a village which has long been associated with the linen firm of John Shaw Brown & Sons Ltd. This firm had a convenient quay for the discharge of coal to their factory. The nearby lock was known as Rosie's, no doubt named after Rosie Ward who acted as its lock-keeper around 1834. The name of Ward, like that of Kilpatrick, was almost synonymous with lock-keeping on the Lagan for many years. The name Norwood

was also associated with this (and the next) lock in the mid-nineteenth century, but the last recorded lock-keepers at No. 4 were Tommy Singleton and Thomas Rea.

The second lock on this stretch was Ballydrain, manned by Robert Norwood around 1880, and, more recently, by James Smyth, James Gallagher (who could play the fiddle a treat), Dick McClelland and Robert H. McDowell. Not much is known about this lock, though it is recorded that on 4 December 1851, 'the widow Herron paid one shilling for the privilege of grazing her cattle along the towing path between the fifth and sixth locks at Ballydrain'. On this stretch a metal bridge (formerly a stone bridge) crossed to the island formed between the river and the canal. It was known as the Chimney Bridge and accommodated a local farmer in taking his cattle to graze. It is in this area that the trees are at their loveliest and the sense of peace and seclusion at its greatest. A walk on the towpath here on a summer evening is a treat indeed; though not to the canal man. As he passed Ballydrain, the pace of the hauler would automatically quicken, for according to tradition, strange influences hung about the place and at least one seasoned lighterman admitted that he always experienced a feeling of chill and darkness there, even on a warm summer day. The only one who actually saw anything was a lighterman called Paddy McCaugherty and to his dying day he would never disclose what he had seen. An apparition of some kind it must have been, for he was so strangely affected that he was never quite the same after it. Small wonder then that no lighter ever stopped overnight on this stretch of water. It always kept going till it reached 'the Drum'.

The Drum, or Drumbridge, was the sixth in the series of seventeen locks leading up to the head level, and the fourth one to be situated in an artificial cut as opposed to the river itself. In its early days it was manned by the Ward family but its last lock-keeper was Matthew Irvine who reigned there for half a lifetime, succeeding Samuel Eccles, Theo McCord and Samuel Basset. Matthew kept a dozen or so Nubian goats which were inclined to stray off into the trees in search of fresh pastures, and which he summoned at milking-time by ringing a bell. If the coast was clear, it was quite usual for a lighterman or hauler to catch one, and quietly strip enough milk into a tin can for his cup of tea. Goats' milk was reputed to discourage the dreaded tuberculosis.

One of the most interesting features at Drumbridge is the lovely old lock-house, one of several designed by Thomas Omer, the Dutch

No. 7 lock, Mossvale, taken in 1924.

J.L
28.12.25

No. 8 lock, Ballyskeagh, in 1925. Notice the
lighter discharging coal in the 'lay-by'
background left.

Pulley on the wall at Drumbridge. This was the device which guided the rope when a lighter passed under the bridge.

The original lock-house at Drumbridge, designed by Thomas Omer. This is the only one of Omer's lock-houses still lived in, although a number have survived.

engineer responsible for the first section of the Navigation. Omer's houses were built to a distinctive two-storey pattern with a semi-circular arched recess on the ends and front. The house itself is almost square in shape with a huge keystone above the door. Local opinion has it that at one time this house was the subject of a law suit between the Lagan Navigation Company and the Dixon Estates. The Navigation Company is said to have lost the case and was ordered to vacate the premises. Whatever the reason, it is a fact that the lock-keeper and his family moved across the road to a lime-washed cottage which was much more convenient to the lock.

Another interesting relic at Drumbridge is the metal pulley which can still be seen on the parapet wall. This was the device over which the rope passed as the barge went under the bridge and the horse over. Here also the towpath changed once more to the opposite side of the water.

Just above Drumbridge, the canal rejoins the river, but soon leaves it again as it continues towards Lisburn on an independent channel. The stream ' 'twixt Leamh-beag and the Drum' will long be remembered in the words of that lovely old song 'My Lagan Love' (see p. 95). There were five locks on the four-mile stretch from Drumbridge to Lisburn: at Mossvale, Ballyskeagh, Lambeg, Hilden and close by the factory of Wm. Barbour & Sons Ltd.

The first of these, at Mossvale (No. 7 along the line from Stranmillis) was formerly called Agnew's Level Lock and also McQuiston's, once more giving a clue to the identity of early lock-keepers. Nearby are the ruins of its sandstone lock-house, now overgrown and derelict. The eighth, at Ballyskeagh, was usually referred to as the 'High Bridge', its tall sandstone arches carrying the country road from Lambeg village to Drumbeg. A story is told that it was from this bridge that the last man was hanged for stealing sheep. Apparently it was a public occasion at which those present were asked if they had any messages for their friends in hell. If so, the condemned could pass them on when he got there!

The names O'Neill and Kelsey are recorded at these locks in the mid-nineteenth century, and a report of 1884 states that a William Ward at No. 8 exchanged places with his son Arthur at No. 7, because 'the heavier duties and long climb up to the lock-house at Ballyskeagh were becoming too much for an old man'. In their last years both locks had a succession of lock-keepers, but they were manned for a long time

J.L
23.12.25.

by Edmund Hawthorne and John Myles respectively.

Beyond Ballyskeagh Bridge, Lambeg Church and village come into view, and below the trees of Chrome Hill a glimpse can be seen of Wolfenden's Bridge which took its name from a family well known in the area for excellence in the manufacture of blankets in the seventeenth and eighteenth centuries. Prior to the building of this bridge, there existed a ford at this spot, and a story is told that when King William III was crossing by the ford, his carriage lost a wheel, making it necessary to call upon the local blacksmith for repairs. This blacksmith happened to be a native of West Flanders, René Bulmer (a name now found locally in the form Boomer) who had come over with the Huguenots. When called to the King's aid, René delighted His Majesty by answering in perfect French, and before resuming his journey the King saluted with a kiss (in true continental fashion) the young and attractive wife of the blacksmith of Lambeg.

It has been said that the linen industry of Northern Ireland was born within the confines of Lambeg Parish. Certainly a bleach green was established there as far back as 1626 by a John Williamson. Another of that name later became known as 'the famous bleacher of Lambeg'. When the Huguenots arrived in 1685 linen manufacture was already a flourishing industry to which they brought fresh methods and ideas. The bleachyards of Messrs Handcock, Barklie and Richardson were renowned not only in the Lambeg–Lisburn area but were said to be amongst the most extensive in Ireland (*Parliamentary Gazetteer of Ireland*, 1846).

One account of Lambeg thought to have been written in the late eighteenth century states that the village at that time 'contained 29 houses of which 20 were thatched, and white-washed with lime both inside and outside'. The same account added, 'The Lagan still affords the parishioners such fresh fish as is common to be found in other rivers, and before the connection with the canal or weirs being put to it, salmon of the best quality was [*sic*] abundantly found in most parts of it in their season'.

Among the many people who looked after the nearby ninth lock were John Kain (or Kane) and Billy Livingston. A William Menow had completed thirty years as lock-keeper there in 1885 when he was reported as being too frail and unfit to carry out his duties.

The tenth lock-keeper had a walk of two hundred yards to reach the lock just below Hilden. Like most others in this area, his lock-house

Another view of No. 8 lock, looking towards Ballyskeagh Bridge, 1925.

was built to Omer's original design, his bedroom being approached by a steep stone staircase and the windows so placed that he could see his lock from almost every corner of the house. Lock-keepers here included in the 1850s a J. Morrison and more recently Johnnie Kilpatrick, Harry Elliott and Billy Hart. To lightermen, the curve just below the tenth lock was known as Hunter's Corner, after James Hunter, who was the owner of a local bleach green from 1741–1781. This was probably the origin of the Glenmore Bleachworks, which had two quays on the wide sweep of the curve. Between the curve and the lock there was a footbridge to facilitate workers approaching from the County Down side of the mill. The road bridge here and at the next lock have had their humps removed in the interests of safety.

The names McAlice, Smyth and McPoland are recorded as lock-keepers at the eleventh lock, usually referred to as 'Scott's' (after Wm. J. Scott). This lock was situated close by the massive premises of Wm. Barbour & Sons, a firm which once claimed to be the largest manufacturers of thread of every description in the world. John Barbour, a native of Paisley, was the original founder of the linen thread industry in Northern Ireland, and the village of Hilden grew according to the growth of his 'Works'. In the mid-nineteenth century, the neighbouring firm of Richardson, Sons, & Owden was one of the largest linen manufacturing firms in the world, while at Lisburn the firm headed by the Coulson family was famous for its beautiful damasks. The Lagan Valley had, by then, become renowned for spinning, weaving, bleaching, dying, beetling and finishing; in fact anything and everything to do with the manufacture of high quality linen. A poet of the time expressed this thought in these words:

> Here sits industry laurel-crowned,
> With capital and labour meeting
> In union on one common ground,
> Within the world's great marts competing;
> Where Coulson's damask, Barbour's thread
> With Stewart's and the Island Spinning,
> In workmanship the world have led
> High honours from the nations winning.

The River Lagan was a significant factor in the growth of the linen industry though the needs of the linen merchants tended to clash with

No. 9 lock, Lambeg, taken in 1924.

those of the Navigation. The merchants were more powerful and many of them were already established when the canal came into being, so that the interests of the Navigation tended to be pushed into second place. So strongly did the Navigation Board feel about this attempted monopoly of the water supply at their expense, that they passed a resolve in 1793 which stated, 'That no bleacher, nor any person in the employ of, or under the influence of any bleacher adjoining the canal shall on any account be appointed a lock-keeper, or have the nomination of one.'

In spite of this, nearly all the linen merchants in the Lagan valley had a private quay for the convenience of their works. These included in 1929 John Shaw Brown, Charley of Seymour Hill, Lambeg Weaving Co., Lambeg Bleaching Co., Glenmore (2), Wm. Barbour & Sons, Island Spinning Co., Lagan Factory and Pedlow's Factory. These quays were used almost exclusively for the discharge of coal. (A list of these and other quays can be seen on page 118.) Several factories also had their own barges, including Barbour's, whose boats, the *Nellie* and the *Eva*, honoured the names of daughters in the family. In 1880, Barbour's purchased their first steel boat which was made by McIlwaine & Lewis of Belfast.

One factory worthy of special mention, if only because of its unusual situation, was what the Ordnance Survey Memoirs for Blaris Parish 1830–70 described as the 'Vitriol Manufactory'. This was conveniently placed on the three-acre island formed between the canal and the river at Lisburn. The original works were said to be built in 'the castellated style' and 'though situated on the County Down part of Lisburn formed a great ornament to the town'. The works were founded around 1760 by Messrs Thomas Gregg and Waddell Cunningham for the manufacture of the chemical Vitriol and this gave the island its name, Vitriol Island. The premises changed ownership several times and changed to the manufacture of linen and thread when purchased by Samuel Richardson in 1840. He was succeeded in 1847 by his brother J.J. Richardson who greatly enlarged and modernised the premises. The Island Spinning Co. was established in 1867, and in 1882 the production of linen threads was made an important feature of the manufactures. Like several other factories in the neighbourhood its goods found customers all over the world. The twelfth lock, watched over by its adjacent lock-house, was situated in the artificial cut close by the island and, a short distance ahead, a left turn led directly to the

The motor-boat *Nellie of Hilden* at Barbour's Mill. This boat changed ownership several times and each time was given a new name. Other names were *Bellarena* and *Ida* (see illustration, p.52. This is not the same boat as the original *Nellie* owned by Barbour's which can be seen on p.25.

The lighter *Nellie* discharging coal at Barbour's quay. The crane used to discharge the coal ran on a permanent tramway which can be clearly seen in the foreground.

Union Bridge in Lisburn. This was built in 1880, replacing an earlier bridge on the same site. An even older bridge forded the Lagan 95 yards north of the present one. The old bridge was said to be:

of old standing and very narrow and greatly dilapidated when condemned and the above bridge built. It was by this older bridge that all carriages, etc., formerly passed from Lisburn to and from Dublin and also by the present bridge till the New Road was made.

O.S. Memoirs, Blaris Parish 1830–70

Barbour's Mill. The water courses seen here are (left to right) the canal, the river and the mill race which served this and other mills in the area.

BRIDGE ST LISBURN. 1779. W.L.

Union Bridge, Lisburn. Published with the permission of the National Library of Ireland, Dublin.

The River Lagan and the entrance to the canal at the Island Spinning Mill, Lisburn. Notice the bridge and weir in front of the Dye House and Thread Dept. to the left. The boats shown are (left to right) the stone-mason's boat, the maintenance scow and a lighter discharging coal.

Lisburn has always been an important transport centre, being an obvious stopping place in days gone by for coaches travelling west or south from Belfast and claiming over the years not only a main canal but also a mainline railway and a motorway. It was also on the route for North-South traffic wanting to avoid Belfast. Its harbour was one of the busiest on the Navigation system and was the destination of the vessel, the *Lord Hertford*, which opened the Belfast–Lisburn section of canal on a beautiful autumn day in September 1763. However, the scene was not so serene two years later when the people of Lisburn were preparing to receive large quantities of sea-coal via the new canal. On that occasion three boats were loaded at Belfast with from five to fifteen tons each and while the townspeople waited patiently for their arrival, the boats all but foundered in gales and floods at Newforge and did not arrive at Lisburn till all of five weeks and two days later. Carts from Dromore, Dungannon and Portadown had

Advertisement for Millar & Stevenson.

Quay Street, Lisburn, 1974. On the left are the premises of the merchants Millar & Stevenson (formerly Robert Allister). The white building in the centre of the photograph concealed stabling for Robert Allister's horses and behind it was Albert Hanna's blacksmith's shop. The ground floor of the building to the right was used as a coal store, as was the 'Blind Yard' beside it. The loft was used for storing hay.

The fencing posts by the water's edge mark the line of the former public quay owned by the Navigation Company and used extensively by the nearby gasworks for unloading and carting coal.

carried away all the coal before the lighters had left to go for their second cargo. Appropriately Lisburn was also the destination of the last barge, which came to the Island mill in 1954 with a load of coal.

In the days when Lisburn was a busy port, there were nine quays constantly in use at its harbour. One was a public quay owned by the Navigation Company and used for discharging general cargo (including, since 1837, coal for the nearby gas-works), and eight were privately owned. Four of these, along with about a dozen others between Edenderry and Lisburn, were owned by the various spinning, weaving and bleaching mills of the Lagan valley and were used almost solely for the discharge of coal. Two belonged to Millar & Stevenson's who were general merchants. This firm (formerly owned by Robert Allister) was established in 1793, thirty years after the opening of the canal to Lisburn, and one year before it opened to Lough Neagh. Coal was again the main commodity handled and the men who unloaded it were paid at the rate of one penny per ton. The remaining two quays were owned by a Co-operative Society and a corn merchant and were situated just south of Union Bridge. There was also an emergency quay in Hancock Street.

In 1837, a dry dock was erected near the public quay by Henery Mulholland, a Lisburn timber merchant who is reported at that time as owning two lighters himself, one of them rigged for sailing on Lough Neagh. The dock was for the accommodation of building and repairing small vessels and lighters, an accommodation hitherto unknown along any canal or navigable river in the province of Ulster at that time 'except for one in the town of Belfast'. It was said to be big enough to admit two or three lighters for repairs at the same time and was so constructed that loaded lighters springing a leak could be admitted into the dock on four and a half feet of water. An old lighter was brought there for repairs as recently as 1943.

The family associated more than any other with the Lisburn lock was the Hanna family. A John Hanna was responsible for the maintenance of the lock and quay in the latter part of last century and almost certainly would have witnessed the demolition of the old and the building of the new (Union) bridge across the Lagan in 1880. He would also have been concerned with the removal of four old lighters sunk between the lock and pen-weir in 1888 and the dumping and spreading of sixteen tons of broken stones on the quay-side in an effort to fill the holes made by heavy cart traffic. Loaded carts normally made their

Richard Hanna at his lock (No. 12) close to the Island Mill Spinning Mill at Lisburn. The houses of Canal Street are visible in the background.

way along Quay Street into Bridge Street, many of them turning into Herron's Alley with coal for Lisburn Gas Works.

John Hanna's brother James and James' son Richard (known as Dick) were the lock-keepers here for a period spanning almost a century, Dick's stint covering in itself nearly sixty years. Dick supported a wife and four children on his ten-shillings-a-week lock-keeper's earnings and is remembered as an efficient, sincere and well-loved man who was the recipient of no less than three certificates from the Royal Humane Society for life-saving. A newspaper article of that time stated that he had saved over twenty persons from drowning in the canal at one time or other and not only had he risked and imperilled his own life to go to a fellow being in distress, but he had gone into the water on several occasions to save the lives of horses, and in the bitter cold of winter too! At a presentation in 1913 the people of Lisburn gave Richard a purse of gold sovereigns expressing themselves in the following words: 'Not that this is sufficient to express our feelings for the noble part you have acted, but simply to show that noble deeds live in the memory of men, and we all feel proud to have a hero in our midst.'

With so much activity on its waterfront, it is not surprising that Lisburn is mentioned occasionally in verse and song. Richard Hanna's son (another James), all his life a maintenance man on the Lagan, has a favourite song, 'The Lagan Canal', which is a variation of 'The Cruise of the *Callabar*' (see Chapter VI).

By 1765 the river had been made navigable as far as the thirteenth lock and this marked the end of the first section of the Navigation. This was known as Hogg's Lock and for many years its gates were operated by members of that family. These included William Hogg in 1856 followed by his widow Becky, and at a later date Mrs Anderson (née Hogg) followed by her brother Edward. Edward married Mary Kilpatrick, the sister of Alexander Kilpatrick who came there as lock-keeper in 1911, having come from the Goudy Bridge – Anadroughel locks. Alexander lived till he was ninety-two and was succeeded by his son James.

Upstream from the thirteenth lock the Lagan is joined by the Ravernet River, and the nearby Moore's Bridge, built in 1825 at a cost of £3,000, carries the county road from Lisburn to Hillsborough.

Beyond the bridge, a sharp bend in the river (lightermen called it a quick-bend) led directly to the Union Locks at Sprucefield. Today you

The Union Locks, Lisburn. The building on the left is the maintenance shed where lock-gates, etc, were made and repaired. The white building on the right is the lock-keeper's house and stable. The boat in the water is the stone-mason's boat; that on the bank is the ice-boat.

would have difficulty in finding these on a map, yet this now sadly neglected spot was a virtual hive of activity in the heyday of water transport. It was here that the canal finally parted company with the river, a flight of four locks lifting the level of the water twenty-six feet in a horizontal distance of one hundred yards. Between two of the locks there was a basin, a wide place where a boat could make a temporary stop while the lock-keeper was busy elsewhere. A boat-house, a carpenter's workshop, a neat lock-house, several stables and a coal-quay were situated close by. Beyond the bridge (on the Newport side) there was a second quay owned and used by a local farmer.

The horse-bridge which carried the towpath across the river was removed in 1958 and the hump-backed bridge by which the Blaris

Road crossed the canal was taken away at the advent of the motorway. Use of the workshop was discontinued in 1956 as it was on the point of collapse, and access by boat had by this time become impossible.

Steep steps led directly from the locks and past a garden to the house and office of the canal manager. This was built in 1866, has changed very little over the years, and still bears the name Navigation House. It was to this house that George Lynch flitted when he was appointed superintendent of the canal in 1909. His possessions were loaded on a barge at his old home in County Monaghan and brought via the Ulster Canal, the River Blackwater, Lough Neagh and the Lagan Canal to Lisburn. When the barge reached Halliday's Bridge, Hughie Bann (the bank-ranger who looked after the maintenance of the banks on that section of the canal) came on board and on arrival at Sprucefield helped the family to unload their furniture and carry it up the steps to their new abode.

In addition to normal communication by telephone with the first, sixth, Union and twenty-seventh locks, the Navigation Company had a private phone which operated between Navigation House and most of the Company's houses between there and Lough Neagh. The mode of ringing was to ring the number of times corresponding to the number of the station required; one ring for Ellis's Gut, two for Aghagallon and so on. The bell rang in all the houses along the line when a call was being made.

Wilson Ward was the best-known recent lock-keeper at the Union, but James Ritchie and his family looked after the gates there from 1860 till well after the turn of the century. The superintendent recorded that he always found James most careful and attentive in discharging his duties. In addition to opening and closing the lock-gates, these included tidying the manager's garden and acting as odd-job man and general dogsbody around his house. James had a kindly nature and used to turn a blind eye when children jumped on board the lighters on their way home from school. Many a schoolboy fifty or a hundred years ago experienced the thrill of a stolen ride down-river from the Union or Becky Hogg's, then off at the next lock and home 'like the devil' to make up for lost time. To quote one of them, John Leathem, a sprightly eighty-four-year-old when I met him walking the towpath:

> I used as a child to jump barefoot on to the deck of a lighter at Blaris and ride to Lisburn or Hilden. I remember well the smell

Barge at anchor by the coal stores at
Newport.

Nora Ruddy fishing with a bamboo rod by Kesh Bridge. One of the Inland Navigation Company's barges can be seen at the right of the photograph.

The same scene today. The motorway now runs where the canal was and the old Kesh Bridge is no longer.

of the tarpaulins and the warm boards and I sat on the hatch. I loved to sit and watch the horse. The hauler coaxed and swore and muttered as we went along, but truth to tell the horse knew the job better than he did, and could have managed just as well without him. It's sad to think they're all gone.

Once past the Union Locks a lighter was on the 'head level', the first few miles of which have virtually disappeared since the construction of the motorway, but from Moira onwards the canal and its locks and bridges are still there to be seen (see map, p. 127). There were, of course, no locks on the eleven-mile summit level, but there were a number of picturesque hump-backed bridges typical of the canal era. These had headroom of around nine feet at full draught (just enough to allow a barge to pass comfortably underneath). Most of them had a quay or landing place, some had stables, a few had a convenient shop, and some also had a coal store. These included Blaris Bridge, Newport Bridge, Kesh Bridge, Halliday's Bridge, Lavery's Bridge, Beattie's Bridge, Boyle's Bridge, Hertford Bridge, Lady's Bridge and Soldiers-town Bridge.

One of the busier quays was at Newport, from which a trade in grain and coal was carried on to the nearby Hillsborough Distillery. Four lighters, Hillsborough-owned, were plying the canal in 1837. By 1905 this number was reduced to two. They were the *Hillsborough* and the *Newport*, owned by the East Downshire Steamship Co. and skippered for many years by the brothers John and Samuel Taggart.

Like many another place 'down the line', Newport owes not only its name, but its very existence to the development of the canal. At one time it was anticipated that its harbour would be a great asset to both agriculture and industry in the area. To quote John Barry's book *Hillsborough*:

In 1820 or thereabouts Lisburn Street rejoiced in the name 'Great Newport Street' (in those days the canal was in the fore-front of people's minds, and the 'new port' about a mile from the village seemed to be as full of promise as a gold mine).

Industrialisation and building development have altered the Newport–Culcavey area substantially in the 1970s, but previous to this, it still bore many of the hallmarks of the canal era. One was the existence locally of the name 'Puddledock'. Culcavey village had its Puddledock Row (now 7–10 Hart Terrace); Puddledock Road stretched from Newport to the Maze (now Aghnatrisk Road); and Puddledock Farm lay between the Puddledock Road and the canal itself. Rightly or wrongly these names have been discontinued, but like most of our Ulster placenames, they were both meaningful and historic. The 'puddle dock' was the place where the navvies (this word is a shortened and corrupted version of 'canal navigators') dug out the clay and mixed it with water to make a watertight lining for the canal. (A similar dock existed at Bradley's Basin near Aghalee.) When the navvies had finished, there were huge holes where the dock had been, and it was not until a century later than these were filled in by Joseph McCandless, the then owner of Puddledock Farm. Today the farm is known as Laurelvale.

Just beyond the puddle dock was the Kesh Basin, a well-known passing-place, and at nearby Kesh House a coal business was carried on by Paul McHenry, one of whose boats, the *Phoenix*, was skippered by local man James Taggart. Two of James' sons also worked at the Kesh, one shovelling coal out of the boat while the other heaved it to the store in a wheel-barrow. (Hard work, but they were able to move ninety tons in two days.) The coal business here was typical of many another 'down the line'.

It is difficult to know to what extent individual quays were used, but the 'Monthly Return of Lighters' (see p.116) would indicate that approximately one third of all traffic discharged at Lisburn, one third at the head level, and the rest at other destinations.

By far the greatest tonnage unloaded at the various quays was in coal, and boats returning from Lough Neagh usually carried flour, turf, tiles, sand or farm produce. Wheat was widely grown in the nineteenth century, and Soldierstown was one of several quays used for its shipment in bulk to various destinations, as the accompanying document testifies. It was also one of the first to fall into disuse and while other quays were still being used regularly in 1929, Soldierstown is reported as being in ruins. Again it was at Soldierstown (or Hammond's) Bridge that a small boy on his way to school saved the day when a horse fell into the canal. He ran to the nearest farm to fetch help and school was forgotten as he and his pals waited to see the animal brought safely out, harnessed, given a few encouraging slaps and put on its way again as if it were all in a day's work. At Soldiers-

The motor lighter *Ruby* discharging at Kesh Quay in 1933. This boat was owned by the Inland Navigation Company and had originally been horse-drawn. The captain was John Mulholland and his son John was engineman. James Taggart is emptying coal from the tub into a cart while Dan O'Donnell operates the winch. The boat to the extreme right of the picture is the *Patience*.

The aqueduct, which carried canal and towpath across the river near Moira. It was demolished to make way for the motorway.

town, as at all bridges on the head level (except Kesh Bridge), the towpath passed under the arch so that a barge could pass straight through without having to be unhitched.

At Halliday's Bridge and the Broadwater, there were stop-gates, but these were seldom closed except when the head level needed drained for repairs. According to local opinion they were once closed and used as a boom thus preventing the movement of illegal traffic at a time of curfew during the troubles of the Twenties. Near both sets of stop-gates, on the hauling side, there was a house owned by the Navigation Company and occupied by a bank-ranger whose main duties were concerned with maintenance of the canal. These and the stop-gates were erected in 1861. An ice-breaking boat was kept at Halliday's Bridge and another at Boyle's Bridge.

In addition to the road bridges two railway bridges were built in the mid-nineteenth century, one at Moira and the other at Newport. The latter has gone but the one at Moira is still there in its former glory, its iron guard posts notched with the strain of the towing ropes. The nearby Lady Bridge is said to be haunted by the ghost of Lady Moira (whose family left the area in 1763). M'lady usually chooses a moonlit night around midnight, and moves silently about, dressed all in white and carrying a lamp.

The last road bridge to be demolished to make way for the motorway was Hertford Bridge which was formerly close by the site of the present Moira Roundabout. It was from there that Hugh Fox sent a distress call on a wintry day in 1941 when his lighter the *Eliza* sprang a leak, having been damaged by light ice on the canal. Hugh McIlgorm, representing John Stevenson & Co. who owned the lighter, set off from Coalisland with two men and materials for temporary repairs. They found the *Eliza* late that evening, sheltering under the arch of the bridge. Her master had plugged the leak with a pound of Killyman butter (only obtainable at that time on a ration card), and a tin patch nailed over the seam ensured that she arrived safely at her destination.

But by far the most impressive structure on the summit level was a fine sandstone aqueduct, some three hundred feet in length, which carried the canal high over the Lagan just above Spencer's Bridge. It was designed by Richard Owen (the engineer responsible for the Lisburn–Lough Neagh section of the canal) and built between 1782 and 1785 at a cost of £3,000, this sum being met by the Earl of Donegall. The stones used in its construction were quarried at

Kilwarlin on land belonging to the Earl of Hillsborough. Richard Owen's house was also near here and overlooking the beautiful Broadwater, in a quiet corner of Soldierstown churchyard he lies buried. The inscription on his grave-stone reads,

Here lieth the body
of
Richard Owen
of
Flixton in Lancashire
who departed this life
January 13th 1830
Engineer of The Lagan Navigation.

A memorial tablet in his honour stands in a church in his native Flixton.

A good mile beyond the Broad Water, the eighteenth lock marked the beginning of the descent of seventy feet through ten large locks to Lough Neagh. The first six of these (Nos. 18–23) were known as Aghalee Lock, Wood Lock, Sheerin's Lock, Bradley's Lock, the Cairn Lock, and Prospect Lock. For most of the lifetime of the canal these six were operated by only two lock-keepers but in 1906 traffic was so heavy that the superintendent recommended that an extra lock-keeper be appointed to look after the last two. This enabled the first lock-keeper (William Weir) to deliver goods to the store, while the second (Dan Horner) could look after four locks in his absence. Other keepers at these locks included, towards the end of last century, William Ritchie, James Ritchie, Samuel Swain and Richard McCorry, and more recently George Megarry, Richard Green, Wm. R. McKeown and James Agnew.

Close to the Aghalee Lock and Sheerin's Lock, the county road was carried across the canal by a bridge which accommodated a second arch for the horse-track (or towpath).

When coal had been unloaded at any of the several quays in the area, the boat usually went to Bradley's Basin to turn. This basin (or dock) which was close by the twenty-second lock was originally constructed for the accommodation of boats detained under casual circumstances. Almost as important to local people was its suitability for swimming and bathing in summer, and skating in winter. Occasionally the nearby

Quay House Moira, seen through Boyle's Bridge. It is still owned by the Agnew family who once carried on a coal business there. The building reflected in the water was the coal store.

39

The Broad Water, Aghalee. The house in the foreground belonged to the Lagan Navigation Company and was occupied by a bank-ranger. The bank running from the house to the left of the picture was built by the canal navigators to contain the water in this natural valley. The mountain in the distance is Slieve Croob.

level was drained for repairs, which was always the cue for the local lads to wade into it and try their skill at catching fish or eels with their bare hands. One of the more unusual events that took place there was a tub race in which the contestants used spades for oars.

The locks operated by the next lock-keeper along the line (Nos. 24–26) stretched from the Goudy Bridge to just opposite the chapel at Aghagallon and were known as the Goudy Lock, Fegan's and the Chapel Lock. The Goudy Bridge carried a by-road from the Lurgan Road to the Montiagh Bogs and beyond the Chapel Lock the Cranagh Bridge (which was exactly twenty-five miles from Stranmillis) carried

George Fegan.

the road from Whitehall on the Lurgan Road to the village of Crumlin. Like those at Aghalee, the Goudy bridge had two arches, one for the canal and one for the horse-track. The Cranagh had a nearby basin similar to that at the twenty-second lock. This was often used to accommodate a slow or loaded lighter for a few minutes in order to allow a faster boat to pass. Both bridges had a nearby quay.

Fegan's Lock latterly took its name from the family which operated its locks for many years, but previously revelled in the picturesque name of Turtle Dove Lock. George Fegan was the last member of that family to act as lock-keeper and he remembers putting the last boat through with a load of coal sometime during the 1940s. Not so many years before ten or twenty boats a day passed through his locks. George's first task each morning was to fill the Chapel Lock in readiness for the arrival of the first boat from the Lough, and for the rest of the day he cycled the towpath from lock to lock as and when he was needed. During dry weather he shovelled moss against the lock-gates each evening to prevent water leaking away during the night. Shortage of water was a common problem in summer, and George remembers a pump-house and pipes laid along the canal banks in an effort to pump water from Lough Neagh to the higher levels. However the experiment proved uneconomic and was soon discontinued. At the turn of the century the lock-keeper was Alexander Kilpatrick who later moved to Hogg's Lock.

One more hump-backed bridge (Anadroughel) crossed the last mile of canal, and on the southern bank there were two houses owned by the Navigation Company and lived in by the tug-men. A lock, a lock-house, an office and a quay marked the end of the Company's property at Lough Neagh. This twenty-seventh and last lock, known to canal folk as The Gut, was particularly busy early in the day. Not only did it mark the end of the Lagan Canal but it was the place where the bulk of Lough Neagh's traffic converged, as most of it eventually went to Belfast. It was here (as at Molly Ward's) that the haulers congregated at five in the morning in the hope of engaging a loaded lighter for the twenty-seven-mile haul, in this case to Belfast.

A document in the Public Record Office in Belfast states that previous to 1806, 'One Donegan was lock-keeper at Ellis' Gut' (known then as the Lake Lock). Donegan died about 1806 and his widow Polly continued as lock-keeper until 1839 when she was succeeded by Arthur Ward. Arthur signed the customary agreement with the Navigation

Company, in this case worded as follows:

The Lagan Navigation Company agrees to appoint Arthur Ward as their lock-keeper at No. 27, Ellis' Gut, Lough Neagh.

Remuneration as follows – one shilling and fourpence per day to be paid fortnightly. The use of the lock-house and garden. Also the grazing of bank from garden to Cut and from Cut on towing path side to over-fall. So long as he may continue in the service of the company. . . –

Arthur Ward's agreement with the Lagan Navigation Company.

The horse-drawn lighter, the *Charles*, entering No. 27 lock at Ellis's Gut.

After Arthur's death in 1879, Thomas McCleery was appointed, followed in 1897 by Wm. E. Gregg, affectionately known as Eddie. Apart from the duties associated with the lock, Eddie found time to grow enough hay and mangolds to feed his animals in winter. He always transported his crop by boat. Eddie's daughters, Tillie and Emma, lived in the lock-house for many years after their father's death, Tillie performing the duties of lock-keeper until there was nothing left for her to do. Like most canal folk, Eddie, Tillie and Emma are dead and gone. Their last resting place is by the tree-lined path at the parish church of St Matthew in Broomhedge. Eddie did not achieve greatness in the way that the pioneers of the linen industry did, but he too is worthy of being remembered, if only for his life of faithful service to his fellow man.

The motor-lighter *Ida* tied up at Newforge.
The *Ida* originally belonged to the Ulster
Fireclay Works, Coalisland, before being
bought by the factory at Newforge which used
it to transport canned goods to the Belfast
Docks.

II
OF LIGHTERS
AND
LIGHTERMEN

If you'd been along the Broadwater at half past four in the morning, you would have heard them coming, whistling and singing and driving the horse. They were rough but healthy and they seemed to enjoy life. When they went into a pub they would have kicked up a row very fast, but in the normal way they were a fine bunch of men.

George McCartney describing lighter-folk.

Unlike the brightly painted narrow-boats of Britain, the lighters which sailed the Lagan Canal were outwardly dull; most were made of pitch pine and retained the blackish appearance of the original wood. The majority were horse-drawn, though after 1880, a few motor boats were to be seen. The earliest boats were rigged with a mast and sail, for crossing Lough Neagh, for the Navigation Company did not provide tugs until after 1821. The first of these tugs was the Belfast-built paddle-tug, *Marchioness of Donegall*, which had a cruising speed of two knots and had the distinction of being Ireland's first lake steamer. Other tug-boats were launched on the Lough in the course of the next few decades, but the best remembered are the SS *Elizabeth Jane* and the SS *Erne*. The former was built in Belfast and launched in 1876; the latter built in Glasgow and launched in 1893.

The dangers of crossing the Lough were well known to any seasoned lighterman. In stormy weather, the work was precarious (especially if the wind was in the north) and often barges were held up at the canal mouth rather than face the risk of towage across treacherous waters. In 1897 the superintendent of the canal reported that in the fortnight ending 8 September, seventeen boats (the *Erica, Gertrude, Charles, John William, Arthur, May Queen, Snowdrop, Rock, Primrose, Whelt, Lily, Mary Anne, Francis, Perseverance, Cecil, Catherine* and *Ethel*) had been detained owing to rough weather. A similar number was detained later the same month.

Tug with lighter in tow on Lough Neagh. On the bow of the lighter can be seen the crab (or crab-winch) used for lifting heavy weights or as an attachment for an anchor.

Joe Mackell (of whom more later) recounted how in his time four lighters sank in the Lough, one with a man and his wife on board. Newcomers tended to underestimate the dangers involved especially if their previous experience had been gained at sea. Joe told one story about the skipper of a coaling steamer who took up the work of a bargeman and insisted on being towed across the Lough regardless of the warnings of the tug-boat men. This sailor boasted that he had wrung more salt water out of his socks than they had ever sailed in, whereupon the tug-master dubiously agree to tow him across. The sailor's boastfulness was short-lived. The barge had not gone far before the waves were washing over the gunwale. The vessel went under and the skipper would have lost his life had not the tug gone to his rescue.

Lighterman James ('The Jap') O'Neill operating the tiller of the *Charles* as it leaves the Lagan Canal to cross Lough Neagh. Steering a tug-drawn lighter was heavy work because of its speed and the metal pipe James added to the end of the tiller to give better leverage can be clearly seen. The rope served a similar purpose.

Barges were all steered from the rear. Steering a horse-drawn barge was no easy task, for the draught was not at any stage directly behind the horse (since the horse was on the towpath and the barge on the water). It was a skill acquired only through familiarity with the tiller. Canal folk though, most of whom had been born into this way of life, carried out this rivermanship with perfect ease and confidence. Jack McCann, for example, could thread his hundred-ton lighter the *Amy* through the twenty-seven locks from Belfast to Lough Neagh with a precision of timing and certainty of control that had to be seen to be believed. Jack's name was a legend in the history of the canal. He was a fiery man with the reputation of tackling everything with great enthusiasm, a reputation that earned him the nickname 'Hell's Fire'. His lighter, the *Amy*, was built at Portadown in 1906 at a cost of £380 and traded between Belfast and Coalisland in company with the *Lizzie, Mary Ann, Eliza, Favourite* and *John William*, carrying mainly grain and coal upstream; sand, pipes, peat and flower-pots downstream. These lighters were owned by John Stevenson & Co. Ltd., Millers, Coalisland, and were manned among others by Harry Hull, John Maguire, Pat O'Donnell, Tom Bingham, Hugh Fox, John Douglas, Tom McCusker (Tom made good poteen), Wm. Spindlow, W. Watson, Pat McCann, Johnny Hewitt and, of course, the inimitable 'Hell's Fire' Jack himself. Sam Henry in the *Belfast Telegraph* of 6 June 1940 describes how he travelled first-class up the Lagan with 'Hell's Fire'; if a special bag of hay for a cushion could be said to elevate the accommodation to that category! On that occasion the *Amy* was carrying eighty tons of maize from Belfast to Coalisland.

During the nineteenth century the barge was home to most lighter families. A boat surrounded by water can be a cold place, but the cabin was water- and wind-proof and kept warm by an enormous coal fire, which was banked at night with 'small coal' so that a gentle poke would set it ablaze the following morning. Cooking was done on a horizontal metal tray which swung out from the bars of the grate. A larger tray protected the cabin sole (or floor) from falling ashes and coals. Cupboards, one for clothes, the other for delph and cutlery, filled the wall space on either side of the fire. Bench seats occupied each of the remaining walls, with sleeping quarters higher up on a sort of shelf. The table was hinged for easy folding away and the absence of any other furniture ensured that chores were kept to a minimum.

Motor boat cabins were larger and slightly more luxurious. The

Ida's was shaped like a smoothing iron, with the rounded end of the boat incorporated into the living quarters. The table and cupboards were in this rounded end and the hatch and cabin steps at the other; the seats and bunks were on the outer sides. Between the two was a centrally placed small stove, just big enough to hold two pans. A metal rail prevented these from sliding off when the boat was moving. Frugal the furnishings may have been, but with the fire glowing, the scuttle drawn over the hatch and the hurricane lamp throwing its friendly light over all, lighter folk could not have wished for more.

The name Rafferty is one that occurs frequently in the story of the canal. I first met James Rafferty's widow Lizzie when she was ninety-four and when I asked her if her husband had been a lighterman she had no hesitation in answering proudly, 'Yes – and I was a lighter-woman.

'I used to make 'mate' for my family and the hauler, and sit singing. There was my husband Jimmy and Paddy and Frankie that's dead and Lily. Our boat was the *Sara*. She belonged to Benburb and carried Indian corn. We used to go up the Ulster canal to Monaghan, Clones and Wattle Bridge. When we come down the length of George Megarry's I would sing "Here's to the Aghalee heroes" and then Maggie would break her heart laughing.'

I asked Lizzie if it was difficult to mind her children on board. 'I never worried about them,' she said, 'for I always kept them close by me. I used to bath them on a Saturday evening either on the bank or on deck. Then I washed the cabin sole. I didn't allow them back in the cabin till the floor had dried.'

Lizzie raised the first three of her twelve children on board. Those were the happiest days of her life, she told me.

The cabin continued to be home to most families till well after the turn of the century. By then some elected to have a dry-land home so that their children could go to school. Husbands continued to sleep on board only if the boat was too far away for them to come home at night. They didn't seem to mind this way of life. 'It was great', one lighterman told me, 'except for the bugs!' What exactly these were I never found out, but they hid under the floorboards during the day and went into the attack at night. It was useless to try to get rid of them (although some tried by burning sulphur candles) for, according to this lighterman, 'the hauler was back with a fresh flock the next night'. But this was a minor complaint. There is no doubt that the lighterman enjoyed

The young Jack McVeigh on board the *Ida* tied up at Aghalee. The mooring-ropes, sheer-legs and tub for discharging cargo are behind him. The exhaust pipe of the engine is just behind the tub in the centre of the picture. One of the poles at the side was the 'monkey-mast' and was used as a counter-balance while the boat was unloading.

Jane Mullen on board the *Shamrock* in the sixth lock at Drumbridge. The spiked iron attachment at the side of the boat (in the centre foreground) was the cleat and was used to tie up the barge. The mushroom-shaped bollards on the deck behind Jane were used when the boat was being towed. The squarish box behind the water-barrel was the scuttle or entrance to the cabin.

the freedom of it all and if he wanted a diversion when he was far from home, he could tie up at Edenderry and watch the girls flocking home from John Shaw Brown's weaving factory. Alternatively he could leave his lighter at Stranmillis and head off to the centre of Belfast – at the Empire or the Hippodrome he could see a good show for three-pence or sixpence!

Listening to and playing traditional music was another favourite pastime and lightermen and their friends would congregate on board and entertain themselves. The best music-maker within memory was a lighterman called Mosey McIlkenny who could bring tears to your eyes or set your feet a-tapping in no time at all, depending on his mood. Mosey's fiddle was his most prized possession and on one occasion when his boat was in difficulties Mosey was heard to shout, 'Get me my fiddle before she sinks!' The O'Neills (Black Dick and Jamie) were also popular musicians. They played the accordian and could sing and

49

Lightermen Johnny McVeigh and 'Hell's Fire' Jack McCann.

tap-dance (often on deck). So light of foot they were, they danced like paper kites, I'm told.

It was in a lighterman's own interests also to keep friendly with the lock-keeper's wife, for in exchange for the occasional bucket of coal she would keep him supplied with eggs, potatoes and freshly-baked soda bread. He could make himself a good cup of tea any time from goat's milk and Lough Neagh water. The best water was drawn from that part of the Lough where the bottom was gravelled, found where a scan of the shore indicated Maghery Chapel and the demesne on the point to be equally distant. The water there was clear and cool and would keep fresh in the breaker for at least a week.

The movement of a barge is leisurely, reminding us of Kipling's description:

> By the margin willow-veiled
> Slide the heavy barges, trail'd
> By slow horses.

Its pace allowed plenty of time to see everything about, on the water, the bank and beyond. At the beginning of the century, the water was so clear and sweet that both river and canal teemed with fish: trout, perch, rudd, bream, pike and eels. While fishing from the bank was common, the lightermen usually fished with a spoon bait trolled behind the barge. Bob McVeigh caught dozens of fish simply by trolling a metal fish tied to a bit of string on a stick; on one occasion, he claims he caught thirteen pike 'one after the other' as he passed through the Broadwater. Pike were greedy creatures and were reputed to eat almost everything – even pieces of coal have been found inside them. The story goes that inside one eighteen-pounder caught on the Broadwater there was a smaller pike, and inside that pike a rat!

You have only to talk to lightermen to realise how full of canal-lore they were. Jack McCann could have told you in great detail about the habits of water hens and rats, or any other creature that frequented the waters of the Lagan. He said, and swore it was gospel, that when a rat wants to steal an egg, it lies down on its back, taking the egg 'with its four feet', and is dragged home by the tail by another rat. Jack claimed he had actually witnessed this ingenious method of transport. 'There's nothing ould-fashionder than a rat,' he would remark with a twinkle in his eye.

George Kilpatrick, lock-keeper at the third lock.

The *Ida* towing another lighter near the tram terminus at Lockview Road, Stranmillis. On board are Dan and Paddy McVeigh.

A hard existence they may have had but most canal folk would not have changed their lot for any other. Theirs was a purposefully nomadic life. They were born into it and had little, if any, education. For over 150 years they scarcely mixed with non-canal folk, and married amongst themselves. They were a hard-working, hard-living people who left the waterway only when they wanted to escape the cramped confines of the cabin and head for the nearest pub! Some of their favourites were Bob Dugan's (near the Drum), Campbell's when

The *Eva* of Hilden near the Drum Cut. Ned Hanna was the hauler.

they were at the Lough shore, McFall's in the back lane (now Lagan-bank Road), or Hall's at the Union Bridge if they were in Lisburn. A hauler who wanted an excuse could always say that he needed corn or hay for his horse. A bag of corn or a stone of 'whopped' hay could be bought at most pubs for sixpence. Lighter folk generally were a happy and healthy people, and it was not unusual to hear them whistling at their work at half past four in the morning, stopping now and again to shout cheerful abuse to a hauler who didn't 'move into gear' fast enough. They were a proud people too, though there *were* rogues among them. There were reports of one bargeman who was wanted for murder and another who left the country on the eve of the day he was to have married the girl who was expecting his child. His dishonour-able action was not forgotten for on returning to the Lagan community many years later he was shunned by all his old companions.

However most offences committed were not too serious and a lighterman who observed the rules of the waterway had nothing to

fear. All boats were expected to keep to their left or larboard when passing and a boat travelling downstream was expected to give way to one coming up, except in flood water, when the down boat had preference. No vessel was allowed to be moored within twenty yards of a lock, and every vessel by law had to have her name and that of her owner painted in large conspicuous letters on both sides of her quarters. A pass had to be shown before a boat was allowed through a lock and all boatmen were expected to obey the orders of officers of the navigation, including lock-keepers and bridge-keepers.

Occasionally a boatman took the law into his own hands, and on such occasions the incident was reported by the superintendent, and the offender fined or cautioned. Such an incident was reported on 19 August 1857 when Denis Murray forced the padlock of the Ballydrain lock and passed through it without the lock-keeper being present – and did so on the Sabbath Day! For his sins, Denis was fined £1. Denis was still simmering two weeks later when he obstructed the passage of another boat and refused to obey the superintendent's orders. For his second offence his fine was doubled.

Negligence in allowing a lighter to run into lock-gates was a fairly common occurrence. For allowing his lighter, the *John William*, to damage the gates of the second lock on 4 March 1897, Hugh O'Donnell was required to pay the sum of nine shillings, this being the cost of repairing the mitre of the gate. However, his previous good character prevented him from being fined in accordance with the company's by-laws.

Sheer pig-headedness would often lead a lighterman into trouble too. No self-respecting boatman liked to be passed by another lighter, especially if that lighter happened to be owned by the same firm as his own. Often there was an argument and occasionally it would even come to blows before a rival lighter was allowed to pass. Such an incident happened on 14 September 1897 when the *Maud* and *Gertrude* were being hauled through the head level. The *Gertrude* drew abreast of the *Maud* but was unable to pass because of the stubbornness of the latter's master. As a result both lighters were hauled between the retaining walls at Halliday's Bridge, and were wedged there for three hours. The arrival on the scene of the Marquess of Downshire and friends in a steam launch made no difference. Neither man would put his lighter astern and the Marquess was obliged to postpone his trip and turn back. Both lightermen were considered to be at fault and

Motor-lighter in the sixth lock at Drumbridge in 1924. The lock-keeper's hut is on the left; the lock-house (now demolished) is on the right.

Lighterman Jack McCann and Darkie the horse pose for the camera. In the background is Jack McVeigh, a hauler.

both, in due course, were fined.

A similar incident took place near Edenderry a few years later when the master of the *Amy*, who himself had a reputation for pushing his horse and hauler hard, would not allow the *Favourite* to pass. This lighter was carrying urgent cargo and her master had not only obtained a night pass but had also engaged two horses for the haul, so that he could make good speed. All went well until the master of the *Favourite* stepped on to the *Amy* to clear his hauling lines over her deck cargo. The *Amy*'s master suddenly lost his temper, cut the lines and lifted his pump handle, threatening to knock his rival into the water. The *Favourite* was forced to lag behind till they reached Drumbridge – a delay of nearly four hours.

And there was law-breaking of a more furtive kind. Many of the barge-men, particularly some from around the Lough shore, made good poteen, but those that I met were reluctant to talk about it. There was always a demand for poteen in the towns, and in the first half of the nineteenth century it was big business, if a fellow could manage to get away with it. A Lough-shore boatman was in a good position both for making poteen and marketing it, for he could run a drop off in a remote country area, stow it surreptitiously on board, and transport it without fuss to a pre-arranged rendezvous. The arch-enemy of the poteen-maker was the gauger, a member of the revenue police whose job, until their disbandment in the 1850s, was the suppression of all illicit distillation. Needless to say gaugers were a hated and much maligned group of men. In 1833–4, they are reputed to have uncovered 16,000 private stills in the country. (And how many did they not discover?) After 1855 the task of rounding up the poteen-makers was taken over by the Irish Constabulary. Many a drop of 'good stuff' was confiscated by the old RIC at Drumbridge.

Even more furtive was the practice in the 1820s of stealing newly-interred bodies and transporting them by barge from those cemeteries which were situated convenient to the Lagan (two such were at Knockbreda and Drumbeg). With the development of medical research at that time, a demand for bodies made body-snatching profitable and often a grave had to be watched for days after a burial to prevent evil men spiriting away the corpse during the night. Grisly tales were told and retold till strong men quailed at the thought of going anywhere near those graveyards after nightfall.

Of course, lightermen did have a reputation for being easily scared,

The author at that part of the Belfast–Drumbridge road known as the 'Hollow of the Lake'. The lake is just behind the wall on the right.

especially those from around the Lough shore, with the exception of one – Big Harry McCourt from Derrylaughan. Harry had his feet firmly planted on the ground and would have laughed at the idea of anyone seeing a ghost along the canal banks. However not even Harry would have tied up for the night between Ballydrain and Drumbridge. This beautiful stretch of water was believed to be haunted not by one, but by many ghosts. There was the ghost of Galloper Thompson, a horseman who carried his head under one arm while he lashed his horse with the other. The mud-bespattered horse was said to be panting, wild-eyed and all of a lather, and if encountered was said to have a strange effect on a lighter horse. One lighterman seems also to have been strangely affected by the spectacle, reputedly becoming morose and withdrawn. Then there was the ghostly presence that came out from the roadside and walked beside you up the hill along that part known as the Hollow of the Lake (near Ballydrain) where the trees are dark and wet and the air cold and unfriendly. But most astonishing of all was the ghost of James Haddock whose widow was trying to appropriate some property which rightfully belonged to their son. This ghost first appeared to James Taverner, a servant of the Earl of Chichester, as he rode from Hillsborough to his master's home in Belfast. Taverner was scared out of his wits and, instead of delivering the ghostly message to Haddock's widow, as requested, he took to the hills in hiding. Wherever Taverner went, the apparition followed, appearing again and again until the poor man failed away from sheer worry and lack of sleep. To this day the stone on James Haddock's grave refuses to stand upright in Drumbeg churchyard.

There were also reports of ghostly goings-on at the Union Locks, where a horse and hauler had once been drowned when they fell from the narrow horse-bridge which used to span the river there. Several lightermen told me how, many, many years after, they would wake in the dead of night and hear again the frightened whinneying of the horse and the distressed cries of the drowning hauler.

But the strangest story I heard was from Harry McCourt and, as I said before, Harry was not given to imaginings. The year was about 1934. Here is the story exactly as Harry told it.

'I had missed the last tram out to Stranmillis and I was tired after walkin' it. There were about twenty-two boats tied up at Molly Ward's that night. Mine was the upper one, the first one of the twenty-two, next to Shaw's Bridge. The Boat Club was between me and the sluices.

Lighterman Harry McCourt.

Anyway, I went to bed. I wasn't long there till somethin' wakened me. I shouted to Dan Mulholland (Coolie Dan) in the next lighter, "Dan, c'mon quick. There's a woman burnin' in me lighter!"

' "What are ye sayin'?" said Dan. "Away back to her bed. Ye're away in the head!"

' "Not a bit o' wonder," I said. "C'mon t'ye see."

'But Dan wouldn't come; so I went back to me own cabin an' got back into bed. All at once I wakened again. There was the woman burnin' in bed, a red-haired woman. I saw her with me own two eyes. I leapt out o' bed an' ran up on deck. I jumped on to Dan's lighter. Dan kept sayin', "What you're sayin' Harry, it just couldn't be. It doesn't make sense."

'Then John Quinn came from another boat. John listened, an' then he said, "Harry, if yer' as worried as that, sure ye don't have to stay here. You could move to the next lock."

' "A niver thought o' that," says I, "but the flood's too bad to take the boat any length. I could chance goin' up to Mickey Taylor's lock anyway." As soon as I went down to the wheel I looked behind (I usually looked behind to see what way the boat was throwin' the water up. It was a motor boat y'see) an' I cud see somethin' in the water behind me. It floated up from under the boat. When me eyes got used till it I could see it was the body of a woman, a red-haired woman, the very woman I had seen in the cabin. First I saw her burnin' in the cabin, an' then I saw her in the water. I saw her wi' me own two eyes both times.'

Harry related this story with a directness and conviction that contrasted sharply with the marked reluctance of most lightermen even to mention such things. It was as if to speak out might tempt providence to bring some unpleasant experience their way, like that of Sam Taggart who had a terrible fright when a cloven-hoofed creature, rattling chains, danced on his deck one night. Since the barge was tied up at Halliday's Bridge at the time, near to Liza Brady's, it would seem reasonable to assume that the creature was in fact one of that lady's goats, complete with stake, chain and all. Sam, however, remained unconvinced by this theory and could never again be persuaded to sleep on board.

One well-known name on the canal was Tennyson. The Tennysons differed from the usual lighter-folk in that they were a quiet family who kept themselves to themselves but they were still well-liked and respected. William John Tennyson brought his seventeen-year-old bride, Mary, home to the *Tavanagh*, a wooden lighter owned by John Green & Co. of Kinnego. The Tennysons had two sons, Francie and Paddy, who were big men, around six foot four in height and nearly twenty stone in weight. Francie and Paddy often hauled the empty boat themselves, thus saving the ten shillings they would have had to give the hauler and are even reported to have once hauled a loaded boat from Lough Neagh to Belfast. On one occasion a man called Phil McAreavey had a difference of opinion with Francie. Being a man of deeds and not of words, Francie lifted Phil bodily and pitched him into the canal!

When their father died the two sons looked after their mother well while still carrying on the family tradition of boating on the canal. Even when she became so disabled that she was barely able to manage the short flight of steps from the deck down to the cabin she continued to live on the *Tavanagh*. Then one day Mary became ill. The doctor was sent for. The news was bad and her sons decided to take the boat up to the last lock at Lough Neagh where Emma and Tillie Gregg lived with their father, the lock-keeper. Mary Tennyson's voice was barely a whisper as she spoke to Emma: 'I haven't been well. When Dr Johnston saw me in Lisburn he shook his head and said there was very little he could do. I know I am going to die. I am not leaving here till it is all over.'

The Gregg family did all they could for her, attending to her few simple needs. Then her nephew, Paddy O'Donnell, came along in his boat and tied up alongside the *Tavanagh*. A few days later Mary Tennyson passed away. Relatives were notified and came to pay their last respects. The funeral took place from the lighter to Maghery Churchyard. Afterwards the funeral party had tea with the Gregg family in the lock-house at Ellis's Gut. So ended the life of a grand old lady on the Lagan Canal.

Joseph Mackell was also a lighterman of the 'Tennyson' era. Joe was born on board in the 1850s and was featured in a newspaper article of 16 April 1929. At that time he was over seventy and was in charge of the *Edna* which belonged to William Clow of Portadown. As a boy he did not attend school, except when his father's barge was laid up in harbour, and only then if his services could be spared. At the age of sixteen, he was himself in charge of a lighter. In his latter years, Joe lived alone on his barge, did his own washing, mending and cooking

Attie and Jane Mullen with John McNulty
(centre) on board the *Charles*.

and in his spare time pursued his favourite hobby, wood carving. His only tool was a pen-knife. Joe's dog was his chief companion and an essential member of the crew for he had other animals on board which were not welcome. He admitted to having had the company of rats during his sleep. (Surely the stuff that nightmares are made of.)

A contemporary of Joe's was Arthur McShane who assisted on the lighter *Bessie*. Like Joe, Arthur could neither read nor write. As he himself put it, the pen he got in his hand was a barge pole! The *Bessie* was one of eight lighters plying the Lagan for the old established coal firm of Millar & Stevenson Ltd., Lisburn. Others included the *Annie, Ino, Lily, Maud, Newport, Wm. George* and *Lagan*. The last mentioned was the pride of the canal and the pride of her master, Captain Dolan (or O'Donnell). Instead of the usual steel bands on the water barrel and funnel, the *Lagan* had brass bands which were polished every day. Her cabin was spotlessly clean with its narrow bunk and makeshift bed for the hauler. Near the black coal-fired cooking range was a drawer for toll-tickets. Almost as important to her master was the 'monkey-box', a wedge-shaped drawer for metal polish and cleaning gear. Above the well-scrubbed table was an old-fashioned oil lamp with a reflector and wick.

In more recent years, James Spindlow and his brother Billy became well-known for feats of endurance that were the talk of the waterway. James was the lighterman who skippered the lighter *Lizzie* on the occasion when she was towed from Stranmillis to Carrickfergus to collect sixty tons of salt. He handled and stowed the sixty tons himself in three hours, and was towed back to Belfast on the next high tide. When asked afterwards how he felt, James said he was fine but his joints were stiff! James was, however, better known as the skipper of the *Industry* (owned by the Lambeg Bleaching and Dying Co.) which once made the voyage from York Dock in Belfast to Coalisland in a record time of fourteen hours. As the *Industry* was a motor boat she was not delayed by having to wait for the tug on Lough Neagh and her master had obtained a pass for travelling by night.

Some of the older couples continued with the old way of life right up to the 1930s. These included the Tennysons and both Mullen families, John and Agnes, and Attie and Jane. Attie was a lighterman with R. Stewart & Sons of Coalisland and in his early days skippered the *Mary Ann* and the *Charles*. In later years he purchased his own boat, the *Shamrock*, from John Kelly, a coal merchant in Belfast. This boat had previously plied the waters of Belfast Lough and when Attie arrived at Stranmillis he discovered that, because of its width, it was impossible to pass it through the first lock. However, after a few adjustments, including the removal of the rail from the front and sides of the boat (see picture), this problem was solved. Attie was a big man who chewed tobacco when he wasn't smoking a pipe. He was considered a difficult man to work with, always impatiently urging the hauler on: 'Keep movin'. What's keepin' ye man? Give 'er the whip. Get 'er movin'.' At this point Attie would suggest an extra half-crown for the hauler if he could pass the lighter just ahead; 'whip' money he called it.

One winter's evening a few friends were gathered as usual into Gregg's lock-house at Ellis's Gut. The weather was wild and wet and it was generally agreed that no boats would cross the Lough that night. Talk centred around former storms and how merciless the waters of the Lough could be. However Tillie Gregg, the lock-keeper, was keeping an eye out, just in case. Her sister Emma recalled how seven young friends had once set sail from the neighbouring Kinnego and how all but one had drowned when a huge wave swamped their yacht on the return trip. As darkness began to fall Tillie spied the tug-boat in the distance, a lone figure visible on the deck of the one lighter in tow. When it came nearer she recognized the notorious Attie, who, ignoring Jane's and the tug-master's protests, had strapped himself to the tiller and insisted on making it to The Gut that night. He had survived the crossing (as he knew he would) and now sailed triumphantly towards the shelter of the canal mouth.

Attie was, of course, a good boatman and he and Jane made a good team in spite of their arguments and quarrels. Attie normally steered, only entrusting Jane with the tiller when he felt the urge for a smoke. Jane usually went below to fetch the pipe, filled and lit it and surreptitiously snatched a few puffs herself before handing it over to Attie. It was common knowledge that she enjoyed a smoke too!

Jane was a rather large woman with a homely face and even homelier figure. Her clothing in winter was thick and warm, for many a storm she faced on the Lough or on the canal. Her size and manner possibly daunted some, but underneath she was not so formidable at all. Jane's human side is demonstrated in a lovely story told by Lizzie Rafferty. On the day when Lizzie's first child Frankie was one year old, Attie and Jane arrived into her cabin with a brown paper parcel. In her usual forthright way Jane opened the parcel herself and pulled out a blue dress which she insisted on putting over the protesting child's head there and then. (In those days boys wore dresses to hoodwink the fairies into thinking they were girls and therefore not worth stealing.) When Frankie eventually escaped he delighted his audience by taking his first tottering steps across the cabin sole into Attie's outstretched arms.

On another occasion (the year was about 1930) Attie's boat was in Dan Horner's lock at Aghalee being passed through to the next level when Bob McVeigh's lighter crashed into the lock-gates, bursting them open and emptying the lock-chamber of water in an instant. Down went the *Shamrock* with a thump. Jane (who was in the cabin making Attie a bite to eat) must have thought the 'End' had come, when she was so unexpectedly thrown across the cabin sole. However, frightened though she undoubtedly was, she picked herself up and scrambled on deck to demand an explanation. To quote Susan Agnew, the lock-keeper's granddaughter, who remembers the incident well:

'She jumped off the lighter out on to a willow tree that was lying on the bank. She was trembling like a leaf, poor soul. We brought her into the lock-house and made her a cup of tea. She could hardly drink it for the trembling in her hand. She kept saying, "I'll have to go back to the cabin. I've left the pan on." '

Whether or not Attie got his breakfast that morning I don't know but once more he (and the *Shamrock*) came through unscathed. However, it cost £70 to repair the damage done to Dan Horner's lock-gates, and Bob McVeigh's lighter, which had caused the accident, had to be steered back to Belfast with a bent rudder.

When his boating days were over Attie bought and furnished a cottage on the Lough shore, his very first home on dry land, but he missed the old way of life and the business of sleeping in a conventional bed worried him. One day he set to and fixed a bunk across a shed at the rear of the house. He slept the sleep of the just that night and every night after it till the end of his days.

There is no doubt that Attie and Jane were a colourful pair, providing an endless source of conversation and amusement for other canal folk. Attie survived Jane by eleven months and both are laid to rest at Maghery.

A horse-drawn barge near Newport. The
hauler is Arthur Rogan.

III
OF HORSES
AND
HAULERS

I left here in the mornin' an' went to Belfast. That was twenty-seven miles, an' then back. Mind ye that was a long day's dander.
Joe McVeigh (hauler)

Of all the people who worked on the canal the hauler was the least privileged, for by the very nature of his job he was constantly at the mercy of the elements. Summer or winter, rain or shine, he trudged the weary miles encouraging his horse along in a language that only the two of them understood; yet nearly all were happy in their work and when asked about their younger days would answer with pride, 'Aye, I was a hauler in the canal.'

Well-known hauling families included the McVeighs of Lavery's Bridge (Bob got the name of being a rough man with horses); then there was the Douglas family, Vincent, Eugene, Frank, Gerald, Jimmy and Johnny; also the Laverys, the Catneys, the Boyles, the Mulhollands, the McStravicks and the Creaneys. Each hauler had his own fund of stories about his hauling days, all told with a humour that belied the hard existence they had. One told me how he arrived tired at Drumbridge one day and decided to snatch a few hours sleep before continuing the tramp to Belfast. When his eyes grew accustomed to the darkness he could see a huddled figure under a blanket in the corner of the stable. He lay down nearby and slept soundly for several hours. When he woke he discovered that he had shared the stable with a corpse which had been dragged from the river that morning. Another awoke one morning to find that rats had been eating corn out of the bag he used for a pillow. A third was so tired one warm day that he literally couldn't go a step further. In his exhausted state he put his arms round the trunk of a tree and fell asleep on his feet. He drifted back to consciousness to the voice of the lighterman calling, 'Hi, boy, the horse has stopped.'

Yet another hauler, generally known as 'The Brusher' was often drunk, but his grey mare, Molly, knew the job so well that she was able to keep her master on the rails (or should I say the towpath) most of the time. The Brusher, in common with several other haulers, would stable his horse at one of the locks and disappear for hours or even days, not returning till his money was spent. When his wife Margit protested, he would lose his temper and on one occasion swiped the delph from the dresser with the single-tree (the wooden part of the harness to which the towrope was attached – see p.124). On another occasion, to Margit's bewilderment, he brought Molly right into their cottage kitchen. Having weathered these two scenes and seeing the futility of protest, Margit decided that next time she might fare better if she held her tongue. But this would not do either: her spouse again picked up the single-tree, saying, 'There'll be no dummies in my house!' and started to the delph as before.

The work could be very hard, especially with an unsympathetic lighterman. One hauler, Cyril Heaney, particularly remembered how he dreaded working with 'Hell's Fire' Jack McCann, who seemed to think that the hauler needed no rest nor sleep at all. In Cyril's own words, 'He tried to keep you movin' all the time. He was never satisfied. I mind one time I met him on the level near Stranmillis. He had a big walkin' stick over his arm and threatened to knock me into the water with it. Then one night after it, comin' into Lisburn, it was a nice moonlight night, Jack McCann's boat was lyin' at the top of Dick Hanna's lock. He put his head up. "If ye put yer fut on this boat, I'll chop the leg aff ye." I couldn't get the line roun' only be steppin' on his boat. "Well", says I, "we didn't have it that day on the bank. We can have it now on your boat." But when I faced up to him he wasn't just so bad. He muttered somethin' under his breath and turned on his heel and went down intil his cabin.

'In those days I was friendly with a hauler called Joe Lavery. His mare and mine were great mates. One day we put them into Mickey's field at the second lock and off we went to the dog-racin'. When we came back the horses were in the Cat and Dog Home. We had to pay shillin's apiece to get them out and we were fined ten shillin's apiece for lettin' them wander round Belfast.

'Then one winter's night a lighterman called John Quinn and me come loaded to Halliday's Bridge. From there you would have heard the church clock striking the hour. I put the mare in the stable and fell

Hauler Cyril Heaney.

Paddy Creaney.

asleep. When I wakened Quinn was shouting, "Get up. There's the clock strikin'." Now, the clock was strikin' twelve, but he didn't waken me till the last six. I thought it was mornin', so I got up and give the mare her corn and hooked on. When I come the length of Lavery's Bridge, there was a great light in Tom's and there they all were, never away till bed.'

Paddy Creaney remembers his hauling days as clearly as if the events had taken place last week. When I jogged his memory the answer I got went something like this:

'My life as a hauler! God, I used to have some quare times. Them was the happiest days of my life. In the summer time them banks from Lisburn down were crowded with people. Near the Minnowburn at Edenderry, for instance, there was a foot-bridge across the river. The fellas and girls used to come across it to the Green just fernenst the lock and dance to the fiddle or melodeon till bedtime. It was a lovely sight to see.

'From where I used to live, at Milltown, you could've seen the boats comin' across Lough Neagh, five or six in a line. Mind you, when they were loaded, there wasn't much of them above the water; but they were well battened-down. The Lough can be a rough place. If it was rough the boat-man tied himself to the tiller so that the water wouldn't take him out over the boat. The tug-man always had the say as to whether or not they sailed.

'When I spied them comin' on the Lough, I could set off and be at the Gut afore they come in. The haulers always shouted agin' each other for who would get the haul. They would shout, "Johnny McCann has a horse for ye", or, "Joey McVeigh has a horse for ye," or, "Buffer Donnelly has a horse for ye." The lighterman looked round them all and then whoever he threw the rope till, got the haul. When you hauled a boat out, you were entitled to haul that same boat back on the return journey. That was always the routine.

'The first time I hauled, me brother John took me down with a light boat. After that I was on me own. There wasn't much else to do in them days. There was as good money at haulin' as anythin' else. At that time everything was cheaper. You could've bought a new pair o' boots for ten bob.

'You had to have a licence to haul. The licence cost a shillin'. It did for a year and then you had to renew it.

'It didn't take a classy horse to haul boats. If he was a bit rough he

LAGAN NAVIGATION CO.

No. *C 7*

Belfast, ‒1 JAN 1936 19....

To Lockkeepers and all other Servants of the Company

John Lavery.

of .... to be allowed access to the Company's property for himself and horses for the purpose of carrying out any contract he may make with the Owners or Masters of Vessels using the Canal for hauling Lighters in that portion of the Canal situate between.......... *Belfast* and. *Lough Neagh*

The Company reserves the right to withdraw this permission at any time. This authority, if not previously revoked by the Company, will hold good until 1 DEC 1936

For the Lagan Navigation Co.

HENR ‒ E REA ....Secretary.

Fee £ –:1:0

A hauler's licence, issued by the Lagan Navigation Company.

done all right. You nearly always bought a horse that wouldn't work on the land. What he wouldn't do on the land, he done on the bank. He had it to do, or else fall intil the water. He got that he walked off the square with the boat bein' on the water and him on the towpath. Y'see the pull was all on the one side, the side away from the water; but the traces had wooden rollers to save his skin. Ordinary traces would've cut his flesh. He soon got used till it; and then with the load bein' on the water, if he wanted to stop for a chow, sure the lighter went on! You paid maybe a fiver for him. Sometimes he would have kicked you, maybe ate you forby. But your eye was your merchant. If the price didn't suit, well, you weren't compelled to buy. You brought him home and took a chance.

'Joey McVeigh and me, we once bought a mare from Montgomery in Portadown. She'd killed a man afore it. She would have kicked you for puttin' the winkers on. She would have kicked the stars out of the sky! Montgomery said: "If ye can go up the street and get her out, you can have her for four poun'." *Four* poun'! a poun' a leg! We went and got a handful of carrots and she ate them out of my hand. We took her out and brought her home.

'She went with whistlin'. When you wheeped she stopped. When you double-wheeped she went on. She knew every wheep and she knew every door. There was a door at the foot of Bridge Street in Lisburn where they used to come out and give her bread. When she came near it she pulled on, no matter if you blew your throat out. She wouldn't stop till she reached that door. Then she hit it a thump with her head, an' when they heard her they give her the bread. Sometimes instead of crossin' the bridge she would take off till the waterin' trough in Young Street. Then at the top of Bridge Street there was a butcher's shop, Mayne's – the best butcher's shop in Lisburn. I could have bought a feed of sausages and steak there, and six soda farls, and had tuppence out of half-a-crown.

'In the summer time, on a good night, you slept on deck. You had your bag with a couple of stone of corn in it ready for the horse the next mornin'. You put that under your head and your coat on top of it. You took your boots off and lay down under a couple of oul' blankets you carried with you. In winter, you got sleepin' on the cabin sole. If it was a light boat you put newspapers down first, to keep the draught from blowin' the stour round ye. The hatch was nearly always open at the top, you see. The lighterman would have had a good fire in the evenin' and banked it up at bedtime. That kept the heat in you till mornin'. Many a time you got wet. You took your coat off and dried it. The next day, away you went and got wet to the pelt again! But the sleepin' accommodation was grand. There was nothin' wrong with it! You slept three or four hours. Then the boatman got you up again at scrake of day (maybe four in the mornin'). At night you went till you reached a stable. Sometimes you just put your horse on the grass and jammed somethin' across the towpath at the bridge. The next mornin' you got him either at the bridge or back at the lighter for his feed. If you hadn't jammed somethin' across, he might have walked home by himself in the night.

'It took my black mare twelve hours to haul a light boat from the Gut to Belfast. It took two days to haul one that was full. You got two poun' for haulin' a loaded boat, ten shillin's for a light one. If it was a load of peat, it was lighter and you only got thirty-two shillin's. A load of peat weighed about forty ton. It nearly always went to Graham of Belfast for beddin' horses. Sometimes you could have done three load in a week, but if it took a month the money was just the same... The boat-man paid the hauler... Sometimes the water was that low, and it took the horse that long; you would have gone for eight hours afore you stopped; and then you got the heel of a loaf and a mug of tay. If you got to the head level, sometimes you worked all night in the moonlight and got no sleep. You see, you had eleven mile of water there till you reached Aghalee.

'At some places the towpath changed to the opposite side of the water, at Shaw's Bridge for instance, and Drumbeg, and Lisburn. At the Union Bridge in Lisburn, there's a lamp with dogs' heads on it; thonder at the end of the bridge. When you came that length you had to catch the rope in one hand and sling it over. It took you to be quick to be ready to drop it down to the boatman comin' through on the other side.

'Comin' up to a lock, you put your hands to your mouth and blew to get the lock-keeper out. Sometimes you cracked your whip. You did that when you were comin' into a bridge too, to let the other fella know you were comin'. He could lie back then and wait. Some of them had horns but most of them at the last just hollered. When you came to a lock you had to run like hell all the time. You left the horse, shut the lock-gates, drew the sluices, ran and pushed the lock-gates open, back to the horse, always on the move, backwards and forwards, just

The base of the lamp-post on the Union Bridge, Lisburn. The hauler had to swing the towrope above his head at this point and then throw it round the back of the post. Sometimes it caught on one of the animals' heads, making him swear.

Time off for horse and hauler – Joe McVeigh
of Aghalee and Peggy, his trusty steed.

hoppin' about like a two-year-old, goin', goin' all the time.'

Such was the life of a hauler!

Joe McVeigh was born and reared at Aghalee within a stone's throw of the canal. His father worked as a boatman on one of the lighters and when Joe was young, he used to go down to the nearby lock when the boats were tied up for the night and listen to the boatmen talking about faraway places like Mossvale, Wilger's Well and the Bathing House Bight.

As Joe grew older it seemed natural that he should want to see these places for himself. Although Joe's father had been a boatman, Joe was keen to have his own horse, and work as a hauler. Money was scarce in the 1920s and he knew he would have to earn the price of the horse himself. As luck would have it an opportunity to do so presented itself almost immediately and Joe was hired to a farmer at Ballyutoag. In six months' time he had saved the £2.10s.0d. needed to buy a cart-horse from a neighbouring farmer.

A hauler who had not previously been engaged by a boatman usually went to look for work at either the Belfast end of the canal (Molly Ward's) or the Lough Neagh end ('The Gut'). It was at these places that the lighters arrived on the line of the tow, in the case of Molly Ward's usually loaded with coal or grain and at the Gut usually loaded with peat or sand. Since Joe lived just a few miles from the Gut, that was where he normally started.

One particular May morning Joe and his horse set off at four o'clock. It took an hour for them to cover the distance at walking pace from his home to Lough Neagh. By five o'clock he had taken his place among the other haulers who were already jockeying with each other for the custom of the boatmen. When a boatman had decided which hauler he wanted he threw out the tow-rope, the hauler caught it, quickly hooked it on to the 'single-tree' and set off immediately.

Joe was lucky. He was hailed immediately by Johnny McStravick, a lighterman bound for Belfast with a load of sand. In a matter of minutes he had left Lough Neagh and Eddie Gregg's lock behind. Joe knew that if he was first away, he was off to a good start for Ned Fegan would be waiting for the first man to arrive at the Chapel Lock. Ned looked after three locks (Nos. 24, 25 and 26), from the chapel at Aghagallon to the Goudy Bridge. When Joe started at the Lough Neagh end of the canal he was actually working through them in reverse order.

As Joe expected, Ned was watching for him and in a few minutes he had passed through to the next level. Ned then pedalled off on his bicycle to make the next lock ready before Joe and his horse reached it. The hauler coming behind Joe was not so lucky. He had to do his own lock-keeping as Ned passed Joe through all three of his locks before returning to the first one. Dick Green, Dan Horner and George Megarry, the next lock-keepers along the line, looked after Joe in the same way.

By this time it was midday and both horse and hauler were ready for a bite to eat (in summer the horse grazed the banks, and in winter ate hay or oats from a nose-bag) but there was no time to lose and soon they were on their way again. When they came to the 'showl' (shoal) Joe slowed down to allow the lighterman time to inch his way through the shallow water. As they approached the Broadwater, Joe glanced briefly at Arthur's Bush, a small but splendid whitethorn. Why it had been singled out for special attention he wasn't quite sure but woe betide the man who interfered with it.

By early afternoon they had passed through the stop-gates at George Weir's and into the Broadwater. The horse needed careful handling here where the towpath cut off an awkward loop of water by means of a narrow embankment ('the narra' pad', Joe called it). Joe's horse was blinkered, but if frightened it could stumble and fall into the water. This had once happened to Joe so he trod very carefully indeed. Just here the water was black and forbidding and had come to be known as Hell Hole.

As they left the Broadwater behind Joe relaxed for there were no locks on the eleven-mile head level. They passed under several bridges, by-passed a couple of coal quays and then crossed high over the River Lagan on the aqueduct, having seen Barney's Basin and Boyle's Basin en route. By the time they were within sight of Twigger's Corner, a wide place where one of the feeders joined the canal, they were thinking about something to eat again. In a few minutes they reached Lavery's Bridge where they made their second halt. Johnny, the lighterman, took himself off to boil the kettle and butter soda bread while Joe, like any good horseman, attended first to the needs of the horse before joining him in the tiny cabin.

Not far from Lavery's Bridge, they passed a spot called the Reed-maker's. Here there had once lived a craftsman who made up reeds for

The Lurgan Road Bridge near the nineteenth lock was one of several in the Aghalee-Aghagallon area with a second arch for the horse.

The Union Locks, Lisburn.

hand-looms. The next landmark of note was Halliday's Bridge with its feeder making another wide passing place just where it joined the canal. At the back of this bridge there were stop-gates but these were seldom closed unless the head level needed repairs. This was one of those bridges which had a stable, a lean-to effort constructed of wood against the wall and also a shed where farmers could store their produce prior to loading it on a boat. Nearby was a neat brick house where Joe was greeted by Hughie Bann (Hugh Bann Lavery), the bank-ranger on this part of the head level.

Anthony's Corner, named after Anthony McAteer, came next. Long before they reached it they could hear Liza Brady calling her animals by name. Liza lived in a one-roomed hovel near the canal bank and her goats and dogs were the terror of the countryside. Although Joe enquired after her health she gave him but a passing glance for she was more concerned about whether or not there was a coal barge coming the opposite way. The bargeman might throw off a few coals along the towpath as he passed.

This was followed by a straight stretch of canal passing the Kesh Bridge, the Kesh Basin, the Head of the Long Kesh, Dickson's Over-fall, Newport Bridge and McBride's Moss. At Dickson's Overfall the water spilled across the towpath and Joe's horse seemed to enjoy splashing through it.

By nightfall they had reached the Union Locks at Sprucefield and their day's work was almost at an end. Wilson Ward, the lock-keeper, came forward to check the depth of the boat in the water and compare it with what had been written on the ticket issued at Ellis' Gut. A discrepancy would have indicated that the boat was leaking or that the load had been tampered with. Wilson was a quiet man who carried out his daily task without fuss.

Michael Kidd, the canal manager, also lived near here and Frank Russell, the horse vet, lived about half a mile away on the Hillsborough Road. Michael Kidd was on the look-out (as usual) to see if anyone was breaking regulations by travelling after the hour of 9 p.m.

On this particular night Joe did not share the comforts of the cabin for he knew he would be dry and warm in the stable. He removed his well-worn boots, dossed down on his mattress of straw and laid his tired head on his bag of oats. To-morrow they would make it to Belfast. 5 a.m. would soon come and with it the beginning of a new day.

James Hanna and Armstrong Hamilton on
board the steam-dredger. On the left is the
boiler house and on the right the engine.

IV

MAINLY
MAINTENANCE

Lighters made up the bulk of the traffic on the canal but there were other craft which plied regularly between Belfast and Lough Neagh. Most of these were concerned with maintenance and included the inspection boat, the scow, the dredger and the ice-boat. All except the inspection boat were purely functional, each playing its own particular part in the continuing job of keeping the canal in good working order. The dangers of neglecting maintenance can be seen in the following extract from the Ordnance Survey Memoirs for the Parish of Blaris (1834–60).

> Previous to 1830 the canal between Belfast and Lough Neagh was in several parts rendered unsafe and difficult for lighters to pass through by the filling in caused by the collapse of banks of clay, sand, etc., which closed the passage to a great extent. The locks and flood gates were also neglected and let fall into disorder. It was not unusual at that time for lighters to be from one to three weeks going from Belfast to Lough Neagh and back but the interest the Navigation Company have taken in the canal since the above period in making the aforementioned improvements on it has not only rendered the passage quick and safe but has also increased trade and vessels on it.

The most dreaded hazard on any canal is the breaching of its banks. This rarely happened on the Lagan Canal, but after the snow, ice and floods of the 1937 the banks did burst at Stranmillis. Lighters were swept over the overfall and landed at the King's Bridge and Gas Works lock. Fortunately this happened at full tide so the barges were not damaged and all the lighters loaded with grain were able to discharge on to lorries, with the loss of only a ton of maize.

Maintenance could be a controversial issue. In 1925 a disagreement

Workman's scow with pile-driving machine
(for hammering stakes, posts, etc.) on board.

The lighter *Ruby* in Lisburn dry dock. On board is Danny Kerr who repaired the boats for Craigs, the owners of the dock. The arms of the one set of lock-gates can be seen behind the lighter.

of twelve years standing between the Lagan Navigation Company and the Lambeg Bleaching, Dyeing and Finishing Co. Limited was finally settled in the House of Lords. The dispute arose when the Navigation Company raised the height of the gates and walls of the eighth lock and constructed mounds of earth around it to maintain a depth suitable for boats with a 5ft 6in draught. The Bleaching Company objected to this on the grounds that it caused flooding on their lands thus contaminating their dams and filter beds. (Many of the photographs in this book were in fact used as evidence by the Lambeg Company.) The hearing lasted five days and resulted in victory for the Navigation Company, whose case was strengthened by a former Act of Parliament which empowered them 'to repair, maintain and uphold all such works as should be requisite and convenient for maintaining the canal for navigation'. Drainage of other people's resultant flooded lands was a matter for themselves.

The man responsible for overall maintenance was the superintendent (or manager) who was 'the eyes and ears' of the directors of the company. His main duty was to make a weekly inspection of the entire length of the canal and arrange for any necessary minor repairs. He also acted on a once-yearly engineer's report which dealt with major repairs (see p.xx). Everything affecting the interests of the company had to be recorded in his diary and written up in his fortnightly report. (One of these is reproduced at the end of this chapter.) The maintenance work was centred round a workshop conveniently situated near the manager's house at Sprucefield.

The actual repairs were carried out by a repair squad which operated from a flat-decked workman's scow. This had a cabin at one end and was fitted out with a bench and supply of tools at the other. It also carried a forge which was used mainly for making metal parts for lock-gates. Another of its uses was for the conveyance of the materials used in maintenance: timber, iron, stones, whitewash, thatching straw, cinders and sand, depending on the particular job in hand.

A carpenter, a ganger and several labourers made up the main maintenance team, with a blacksmith, a painter and a stone mason. Their work included general repairs to lock-gates, lock-houses, weirs, goods-stores and stables; repairing boats and dredgers; and making wheel-barrows, boat-hooks and other tools for lock-keepers and workmen.

Horse-drawn barge near Shaw's Bridge
(photograph by *Belfast Newsletter* per Dr
W.A. McCutcheon).

Parallel with the work of the scow was the work of the dredger, which carried a team of six men – an engineer and five labourers. Their job was to make up slips in the banks, remove gravel and mud brought down by the feeders and keep all basins and passing-places free of silt. The dredger was usually accompanied by a steel barge for carrying away dredged material. Maintenance craft were usually hauled by the men themselves, unless the distance was considerable, in which case they engaged a horse and hauler.

When their working days were over the scow and dredger were taken to Lisburn dry-dock and broken up but the steel barge is believed to lie in the Lagan near Millar & Stevenson's coal quay.

In addition to the scow and dredger squads, several bank-rangers were engaged full-time in cleaning feeders and drains. The bank-ranger also had the job of removing any bodies found in the water, for which unpleasant task he would earn a small fee. In the Belfast area this varied depending on where the body was taken out. To quote Robert McCurley, whose father was keeper of the second lock, 'If you took the body out on the far side, the inquest was held at Ballylesson and you got two bob [10p]. If you took it out on the Stranmillis side it was five bob and the City Hall.'

The bank-rangers occupied houses belonging to the Navigation Company at Stranmillis, Halliday's Bridge and the Broadwater.

One of the more spectacular craft to ply the canal was the ice-boat which was about twenty-two feet long and made of steel. Severe frost was a serious problem, for it not only made the locks and towpaths dangerously slippery to work on but also caused the canal to freeze over. This happened in the winter of 1937 when twenty boats spent seven weeks stranded at Aghalee. When their supplies and their money ran done, the lighterwomen had to gather their children together and set off on foot to seek food and shelter at the Poorhouse in Lurgan or wherever else they might find it.

Boats were able to push through thin ice but this could damage the hulls of wooden craft. Once the ice thickened, it had to be broken before boats could get underway. The ice-breaker was usually brought out at first light and worked its way methodically from bridge to bridge and lock to lock releasing lighters for work as it went. Depending on the thickness of the ice, it was hauled by one, two, three or four horses, and while they strained and pulled, several men sat in it and rocked it from side to side, holding on to the iron handrail as they did so. The

Ernest Kennedy on board the ice-boat at Agnew's Quay. The iron rail at the side was for gripping on to while the boat was being rocked from side to side to break the ice.

The inspection boat at Ellis's Gut. The building on the left was a store for coal for the tug-boat, that on the right was a stable. The two men on the bank are William Edmund Gregg, the lock-keeper, and James Henry Hill, a bank-ranger.

rocking caused the water to make a wave which in turn broke the ice. The cracking of the ice and the clatter of the horses' hooves on the frozen towpath could be heard at least a mile away on the frosty air.

In contrast, the inspection boat was a genteel affair, though even in the declining years of the canal it was still hauled by horse. At that time William Agnew of Moira supplied the horse and George Weir of the Broadwater steered. The boat had seating all round and a canopy on top to protect its important occupants from the weather. The annual tour of inspection usually took place in the month of May and started at the Lough Neagh end of the canal. In the early days the directors probably made the journey out by coach or jaunting car but in later years they travelled to Lurgan by train. On arrival at Lough Neagh they were ceremoniously received by the lock-keeper, who had had advance notice of their impending visit, and partook of refreshments at the lock-house before starting out on their grandiose tour. The superintendent and secretary of the Navigation accompanied them, the superintendent answering questions and making a commentary as they went along while the secretary made notes and recorded his observations afterwards in a minute book. The party was usually offered hospitality at the Broadwater, Halliday's Bridge and other places along the line. A final lap of honour would have befitted this elegant craft but it was not to be. In 1946, on what turned out to be the last inspection, the boat ran aground in weeds at the Broadwater and the directors had to continue on foot. They abandoned their task altogether when they reached Halliday's Bridge and in their discomfiture turned to that system which had contributed to the death of the waterway – they made their way to the nearest station and returned to Belfast by train! A few years later the upper reaches were officially closed to traffic and for those who lived along the banks a way of life had ended.

Officials of the Ministry of Commerce
inspecting the canal prior to its closure.
Second on the left is Michael Kidd,
Superintendent of Navigation, and on the
extreme right is James Hanna. The boat was
one which belonged to the Ministry and was
also used to tow barges.

Report of C. Magowan. Superintendent.

Lagan Navigation
Lisburn 7th November, 1906

To The Directors of the Lagan Navigation.

Gentlemen,

From the 23rd October till the 6th inst. 72 loaded boats were passed up from Belfast and 71 boats between loaded and empty passed down to Belfast.

The 'Ino' at Ellis' cut from the 27th Oct. till 1st inst. and the 'Thomas' from the 29th till the 30th ult. The 'Charles' at Ellis' cut and the 'Florence' at Newport Trench from 3rd till 5th. High winds and rough state of the lough caused the delays in towing.

The carpenter and his assistants repaired two of the ice-boats and one of the barges. He also repaired and made a number of wheelbarrows and prepared shafts for drags and boat hooks for lock-keepers and workmen.

The fitter was engaged repairing and fitting up the dredging machinery on steam-dredger. This work will be completed by the end of this week, when this man will be paid off.

William Weir and men loaded the scow with cinders at Glenmore and spread it on the towing-path from head of Union Locks on towards Newport. They afterwards loaded the scow and two barges with gravel at Lady Bridge and spread it on the towing-path from Ellis' Cut to Anadroughel Bridge. They are now repairing the thorn fence on the boundary between the Company's property and Mr. Turtle's lands near Ellis' Cut.

Hugh Bann and his helper were engaged cleaning drains near Halliday's Bridge and cutting the boundary thorn fence from Kesh Bridge to Brady's lands.

George Weir and men cleaned the main drain leading through Thomas Beattie's lands to Lagan river near the aqueduct, also a portion of the drain between Boyle's Bridge and the aqueduct.

The water in the summit level now registers 6'8'' on sill at Union Locks and the working draft for boats all through is 5'6''.

David Norwood, lock-keeper at the 4th lock who has been ill and not able to attend the lock-duties for this past three months, and believing there is no hope of his recovery – he left the lock-house on the 27th ult., and is gone to live with a daughter in Belfast. But as she is a working man's wife and not having enough means to support him, he hopes you will kindly allow him a small pension for the remainder of his life which cannot be long.

There are three applicants for the situation of lock-keeper at the 4th lock, viz. David Campbell, grand-son of the late Robert Campbell who was in the Company's service for many years as lock-keeper and a man called John McCormick of Edenderry, also William Mahood of Blaris.

As you are aware Rebecca Anderson who has been in charge of this lock for over 50 years is now become old and infirm and not able to attend to her duties. But she has a brother who has been hauling boats for the past few years and living with her, and who is willing to take charge of her lock duties at 8s.0d. a week. Provided you will kindly give his sister, the late lock-keeper a small pension as the 8s.0d. would not be sufficient to support all. This man, Edward Hogg, is now in charge of the lock.

I am, Gentlemen,
Your Obedient Servant,
C. McGowan.

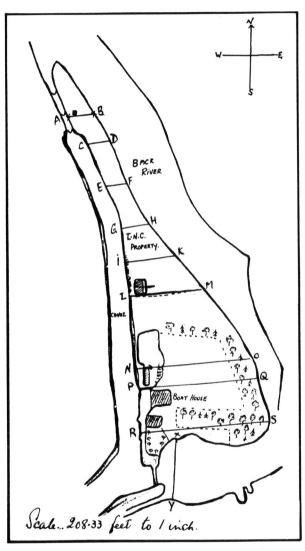

Scale.. 208·33 feet to 1 inch.

Evidence of erosion at the Stranmillis boat-
house island.

Lagan Navigation Company.

C.A.G. GAMBLE,
SECRETARY.

80, HIGH STREET,

Belfast....................... 19....

TELEPHONE: 24141.

Measurements in Feet

Points	1901	1937	Loss.
A – B	83·22	63.	20.
C – D	83.	47	36
E – F	62·49	42	20.
G – H	104·05'	49	55
i – K	187·57	100	87
L – M	291·42	210	81
N – O	395'	343	52
P – Q	416	412	4
R – S	416	400	16.
X – Y	208	239	widened by 31.

Extracts from Minute of Inspection of
11th June, 1946.

No. 26 Lock. The lock-keeper reported that heel post of offside short gate was completely decayed and was lifted out of the socket. It would be impossible to pass another boat until this was repaired. The sheeting on shortgates was leaking badly, and there was a leakage under the sill of deep gates. The masonry coping of lock basin was broken on hauling side.

It was observed that the overfall at head of lock was wasting water.

No. 25 Lock. The heelpost on hauling side shortgate was completely decayed and broken. As a result the motor boat had to be passed through the offside gate.

Lockhouse. Slates on roof require attention. The lockkeeper pointed out that skirting board in sittingroom had collapsed, and the plaster of the front wall would need to be replaced.

No. 24 Lock. Heelpost on hauling side shortgate badly decayed. Heelpost on offside long gate had been spliced. The heelpost on offside shortgate was in bad condition.

No. 23 Lock. Long gate hauling side, ribs decayed. Heelpost rotted. Sheeting of long gates very bad (temporarily repaired with felt). The breast of masonry under shortgates required repair as it was leaking badly.

No. 22 Lock. Mitre post hauling side shortgate completely decayed. Masonry breast work and sills shortgates leaking. Leakages at hollow quoins and also under sills of long gates. Sheeting of long gates decayed.

No. 21 Lock. Swing beam of shortgates hauling side badly decayed. Top rib of this gate decayed. Heel post broken. Sheeting of sills of deep gates in bad order. Sluices need repair.

No. 20 Lock. The sills of both short and long gates are in bad order and leaking badly. The sheeting of all gates requires renewal.

No. 19 Lock. The sills of short gates are leaking. The lock-keeper reported that all the sluice frames would need attention.

No. 18 Lock. There is a fairly bad leakage from the Head Level under the sill of shortgates. The sheeting of the long gates is in very bad condition. The lockkeeper states that there is a bad leak under the sill of deepgates.

As it was impossible to open the shortgates unaided, two of the tugmen accompanied the party to help the lockkeepers to pass the motor boat through the locks.

The hauling side portion stopgate at Soldierstown Bridge was lying partly open.

The lock had been removed from the door of the stable at Boyle's Bridge and the door was lying open.

The sheeting of the stopgates at Halliday's Bridge appeared to be badly decayed.

The lighter 'Ernest' was still aground at Halliday's Feeder.

The bank-ranger's house at the Broad Water,
c. 1980.

V

WILL BEST –
CANAL-SIDE FARMER

At 'The Cairn' Aghalee, there has stood since 1854 a rambling farmhouse, the lovely home of W. Du B. Best, whose family has farmed there since 1804. The proximity of the canal played a significant part in the actual building of the present house, as many of the materials used, including the marble mantelpieces and Bangor Blue slates, were brought on the last stage of their journey by horse-drawn barge to a landing place near the proposed site. The timber, Memel pine from Russia, was imported to Belfast as deck cargo and then tied into raft-like bundles and towed inland by horse. At one time approximately 15,000 tons of foreign timber passed along the canal annually in this way.

The farm, like many others in the province at that time, benefited greatly from drainage work carried out from about 1850 onwards. Few people realise that under most Ulster farms there is a great network of drains which keep the water table at the level best suited to the health of the crops, usually about thirty inches below the surface. Under every acre of land there are about two hundred and fifty yards of drains or seven hundred and fifty drain tiles! These tiles were made at Coalisland and shipped across Lough Neagh by barge. The landlords of the time encouraged drainage by reducing the rent in the year in which the work was carried out.

The canal has long since died a lingering death but it was once a lifeline to the people who lived and worked in the area it served. Although it was already declining in importance before the turn of the century, Will Best remembers considerable activity along its banks in the years immediately preceding the 1939–45 War. Not only was it still used then for transporting heavy goods but it was a popular meeting place for the area's younger folk.

Here in Mr. Best's own words is his story.

'I was born in 1919, just a year after the Great War, on our farm just

'The Cairn', Aghalee.

to the south-west of Aghalee. Our eastern boundary was the canal, an interesting section including half the fall from the head level to Lough Neagh. Adjoining the farm we had the School level, which passed the rear of Aghalee School, the Basin level, named after Bradley's Basin, a wide portion where clay had been dug out to water-proof the canal with puddled clay, the Sandy level, with its milepost saying Belfast 24 miles, and then the Gowdy level, which ended at the lock at the Goudy Bridge.

'Our house is only 200 yards from the canal by footpath across one field – Maghernabree – and when we were small our greatest treat was to coax someone to take us for a trip on a lighter, as the barges were always called. It was easy to hear the sounds of an approaching lighter. The canal people were a cheerful crowd so you could often hear the lighterman or the lock-keeper as they passed on the latest news. We used to watch the clever way the horse would time his pulling to the spring and sag of the tow-rope, and stop pulling at the right moment to allow the boat to drift into the open gate of the lock. The rope would then be given a turn round the red and black painted bollard to check the boat's way before it hit the other gate. The lock-gate was then closed behind the boat and the sluices opened to let the water in or out with fascinating bubblings. When the boat was level with the lock-wall, we would be invited on board for a trip to the next lock. Sometimes if the lighterman's wife lived on board we went down into the cabin with its small coal-fired range, central table and curtained bunks.

'There were a few motor boats then which could be heard a long way off, especially the older ones with paraffin engines. Later ones made a more even noise and one of the newest was a beautiful 2-cylinder diesel. The motor boats were faster and did not have to wait for a tug to take them to their destination on Lough Neagh.

'When I had learnt to swim in Lough Neagh I was allowed to swim in the canal and from then until the War I swam at every opportunity. The Lough end of the Basin level was nearest and a popular bathing place as it had a pleasant rather gravelly bottom. Summer days started in swimming togs with a sprint across Maghernabree, over the stile, up the bank and a running dive off the grass kept short by James Agnew's cows; a swim to the lock, a couple more dives, and back for breakfast. We really felt like a proper breakfast then. Bacon and egg and fried bread tasted very good! Bradley's Basin was a popular place on Saturday evenings too. At that time very few houses had bathrooms

The Best family relaxing after a swim at the Basin level, 1933. The gates of the lock can be seen in the distance.

and the young men used to arrive with a towel and a bar of soap and give themselves a spruce-up for Sunday. The clean-up area was at the far side where the overflow carried the soapy water away round the back of the lock to the sandy level.

'One of the excitements I remember was the approach of the ice-breaker with its two trotting horses making quite a clatter on the frozen tow-path. The crunching and cracking of ice could be heard at least a mile away on the frosty air and as soon as we heard it, we rushed down to see what was happening. I think 1940 was the year when we had a long hard frost, and when the ice was about four inches thick we had perfect skating. On shallow water an inch would be quite enough but with eight feet of water underneath, full of weeds etc., we waited for thick ice before we ventured on to it. On that occasion, we were able to skate into all sorts of places that we never would have thought of, like Bradley's Basin which was rather overhung with trees. Normally it would have been too dangerous to skate there.

'Another of the excitements when I was a boy was the emptying of a level of the canal to repair lock-gates or sluices. All the local boys turned out and waded about with their trousers turned up to try to catch fish and eels in the bottom of the canal. Most of the fish went with the water, of course, when it was drained but quite a number went down into the small stream that was left at the bottom where we could catch them quite easily with our hands. The best time for fishing was the month of March. The pike were in good order for biting then and the canal was still fairly free of weeds. There was always a clear passage along the middle of the canal, the deep part where the barge went. I always fished (or trolled) from the bank. The popular fishing rod at that time was a bamboo pole about twenty feet long and about one and a half inches thick at the butt. J.C. Patterson's of Lisburn kept a supply of these for the purpose and we could have gone there and selected our own. Sometimes we fished with the bait tied to a board which acted as a sort of raft which we towed from the bank with a piece of string. This was also called trolling. The raft, which had a float on top and a strip of lead underneath, was called the otter board. The bait trailed a few feet behind it. We walked miles and miles and very occasionally caught a pike!

'My father often used to tell me of things that happened when he was a boy. He once told me that he and his brother used to catch fish using a rifle. He aimed at the fish, but with the refraction of light the bullet passed just above its head stunning the fish which then floated to the surface. It was then easily caught and brought ashore.

'Another event that took place on the canal in my father's youth was a tub race which was held to celebrate a special occasion, possibly Queen Victoria's Silver Jubilee. Someone suggested that it would be a good idea to bring out all the old wooden tubs that were used for washing clothes in and have a race along one of the levels. They used spades for propelling themselves along. All went well until the very end when the winner overbalanced and disappeared under the water together with the tub. Everyone was very worried, knowing that there was a strong current flowing through the sluices but fortunately the flow of water was slowed down by the tub going over the entrance, and the winner emerged safely at the other side, wet but triumphant.

'Another of my father's favourite stories concerned Dr Duff, who was the doctor in Aghalee between the Wars. The doctor was rather a large man, about eighteen stone, who normally travelled by horse and trap to visit his patients. However one lovely summer day he decided that a cycle-run by the side of the Broadwater would be a pleasant change. He turned his bicycle in by the side of Hammond's Bridge (the one near Soldierstown Church) where the towpath is reached by descending a steep slope. It was here that he discovered that his brakes weren't as good as he thought and he careered down the slope and straight into the canal!

'One of the last uses my family made of the canal concerned my grandfather, who used to go to Belfast every week to arrange with various shops for their supply of potatoes. He was talking to a man who had a haulage business and owned a number of horses. This man told my grandfather that he had trouble getting rid of all the horse manure. There were very few artificial fertilisers in those days and there and then my grandfather decided that he could use an extra supply of manure on his crops, if he could manage to make the necessary arrangements for its transport. He found a lighterman who agreed to do the job for him. Eventually the manure arrived at Aghalee, accompanied by a now rather disgruntled lighterman, disgruntled because he had had to live for several days with the smell of the manure which was noticeable everywhere on board. It took several more days to unload it as the level of the canal was about eight feet above the level of the field and a ramp had to be made for wheeling it off. Some of the willow stakes used to support the ramp took root, and grew into lovely trees about sixty feet high.

'The final operation I remember on the canal was when two engineers came to borrow my canvas canoe. They wanted to take soundings of a cross-section of the levels at different points to decide at what level to leave the water when they closed down the canal.

'There were three possibilities. One was to leave it full, replacing the wooden lock-gates with steel-shuttered dams, and letting the water flow over the top. The snag with this was that the banks would still

Will and Molly Best canoeing with a cousin,
1936.

need to be maintained; otherwise there would be flooding if they broke down at anytime. The second possibility was to leave the water at the level of the upper lock-gate (the lock sill). This would leave a reasonable amount of water in the canal and would also make it posible for adjoining farmers to allow their cattle to drink in the traditional places. The third possibility was to break the lock sill at the upper gate, allowing the water to go down to a trickle in the bottom of the canal bed. This would leave a problem of fencing as cattle would be able to cross the canal from one side to the other – so that was ruled out. They decided to adopt the middle course, and to avoid water flowing over the lock sill, causing damage to the sill through erosion, they filled the bottom with a sloping ramp of stones covered with concrete, and that is how it is today.

'Many years later I had a letter from the Ministry of Finance asking if I was willing to purchase the portion of canal on my side of the canal central line the Ministry to have rights of passage for drainage work and the flow of water. They were inviting all riparian owners to buy their piece of land where the canal had been built. I think most owners accepted this offer. I know I did. Now I own my piece of canal but sadly no longer a canal full of water.'

Billy McMurtry opens the gates to allow the
horse-drawn lighter *Violet* to pass safely out
of the third lock.

VI

'WHERE LAGAN STREAM SINGS LULLABY'

A number of songs and poems have been written about the Lagan. Some are about the river, some about the canal and some about both. This is not really surprising since the canal followed the course of the river (except where the river made wide or awkward bends) until just beyond Lisburn, where they parted company, the canal following a course to the south for several miles before crossing the Lagan by means of an aqueduct and continuing in a north-westerly direction till it reached Lough Neagh. The river, on the other hand, veered southwards and eastwards towards its source in Slieve Croob near Dromara.

My Lagan Love

Of all the songs, perhaps the best known is 'My Lagan Love'. The origins of this song are lost in the shadows of the past, but it is one of those beautiful songs which will surely, like the river itself, go on forever.

> Where Lagan stream sings lullaby
>   There blooms a lily fair:
> The twilight-gleam is in her eye,
>   The night is on her hair.
> And, like a love-sick *leanan-sidhe*,
>   She hath my heart in thrall:
> Nor life I owe, nor liberty,
>   For Love is lord of all.
>
> Her father sails a running-barge
>   'Twixt Leamh-beag and The Druim;
> And on the lonely river-marge
>   She clears his hearth for him.
> When she was only fairy-high
>   Her gentle mother died;
> But dew-Love keeps her memory
>   Green on the Lagan-side.

And oft-times, when the beetle's horn
  Hath lulled the eve to sleep,
I steal unto her shieling lorn,
  And thro' the dooring peep.
There on the crickets' singing-stone
  She spares the bogwood fire,
And hums in sad, sweet undertone
  The song of heart's-desire.

Her welcome, like her love for me,
  Is from her heart within:
Her warm kiss is felicity,
  That knows no taint of sin.
And when I stir my foot to go,
  'Tis leaving Love and light
To feel the wind of longing blow
  From out the dark of night.

Where Lagan stream sings lullaby
  There blooms a lily fair:
The twilight-gleam is in her eye,
  The night is on her hair.
And, like a love-sick *leanan-sidhe*,
  She hath my heart in thrall:
Nor life I owe, nor liberty,
  For Love is lord of all.

Note: The *leanan-sidhe* (fairy-mistress) seeks the love of mortals. If they refuse, she must be their slave; if they consent, they are hers and can only escape by finding another to take their place. The fairy lives on their life and they waste away. She is sometimes called *bain-leanan*, i.e. fairy-sweetheart.

    The cricket (hearth-fly) has always been considered a lucky little beast. Its presence in the kitchen-ends of farmhouses in days gone by was supposed to keep away all evil that might otherwise have entered there. The usual place to find them was among the turf ashes after dark. At one time it was the custom in some parts of the country for a young married couple to carry a 'brace' of crickets from each of the old parental hearths. This was said to bring luck to their own.

My Lagan Softly Flowing

'My Lagan Softly Flowing' is a new song, the words and music having been written by Noel McMaster. Noel grew up not far from the Lagan and spent many happy boyhood hours playing, fishing or just daydreaming along its banks. The result is a pleasant song with an instant appeal, tracing as it does the journey of the river, first through pleasing Ulster countryside and then through the industrial area beyond Lisburn before mingling at last with the salty waters of Belfast Lough. (Any slight inaccuracies may be excused on the grounds of poetic licence!)

1. Early in the morning the sun begins to rise,
    Reflected on her waters, the movement of the skies.
    Slowly she flows onward, disturbed I cannot see,
    Through fields and rolling meadows past local industries.

Chorus
    My Lagan she flows softly from Slieve Croob down to the sea,
     Through Dromore and Dromara, then close to Aghalee.
    From Lisburn down to Hilden, Lambeg and then Shaw's Bridge,
     To Belfast's salty waters where her lonesome journey ends.

2. The years pass slowly onward, changes soon unfold,
    No more horses pulling the barges filled with coal.
    The old lock-gates have rotted, the pathway's overgrown,
    But still I love to her see as slowly she grows old.

3. Oh memories they are precious, and they are brought to life
    As you walk along the towpath in the evening's fading light.
    But even now, the night life begins a brand new day,
    Some ripples on the surface and a trout moves on her way.

4. Young lovers they walk slowly, beside my Lagan stream,
    Holding hands and talking about their wildest dreams.
    Across the water, laughter comes drifting through the night,
    Dancing shadows ripple in the moonshine light.

5. Oh early in the morning, the sun begins to rise,
    Reflected on her waters, the movement of the skies.
    Slowly she flows onward, disturbed I cannot see,
    Through fields and rolling meadows, past local industries.

(Printed by kind permission of Emerald Music Ltd.)

The Cruise of the *Callabar*

George Kilpatrick inspecting an anchor. All lightermen were expected to carry an anchor on board, but most discarded them because of their weight, especially when the water levels were low.

'The Cruise of the *Callabar*' is not intended to be taken too seriously. Again it is an old song with many variations both in words and tune. All the versions that I found relate to the Lagan Canal, but there is a school of thought which believes that these are adaptations of a much older song telling of the first fleet that ploughed the deep from Derry to Strabane. It is my belief that each canal man had his own version which he adapted to suit his own situation.

1. Come all y' dryland sailors and listen till my song.
   It's only forty verses so I won't delay yez long.
   It's all about the advent-chiors of this ould Lisburn tar,
   Who sailed as man before the mast aboard the *Callabar*.

2. The *Callabar* was a clipper ship, well-fastened fore and aft.
   Her stern stuck out behind her and her helm was a great big shaft.
   With half a gale to swell the sail she made one knot per hour.
   She was the fastest ship on the Lagan Canal and only one horse power.

3. The captain he was a strappin' lad, he stood full four foot two.
   His eyes were red, his face was green and his nose was a Prussian blue.
   He wore a leather medal that he won in the Crimea war,
   And his wife was steward and passenger cook aboard the *Callabar*.

4. One day the captain came to me, he says, my lad, says he,
   Would you like to be a sailor and roam the ragin' sea,
   Would you like to be a sailor on foreign seas to roll,
   For we're under orders for Aghalee with half a ton of coal.

5. On leaving the Abercorn basin the weather it was sublime,
   And passing under the ould Queen's Bridge we heard the Albert chime,
   But going up the gasworks straight, a very dangerous part,
   We ran aground on a lump of coal that wasn't marked on the chart.

6. Then all became confusion and stormy winds did blow.
   The bosun slipped on an orange peel and fell into the hold below.
   More steam, more steam, the captain cried, for we are sorely pressed,
   And the engineer from the bank replied, the ould horse is doin' its best.

7. When we woke up next morning we were in a dreadful funk,
   For the mate he had been drownded dead while sleeping in his bunk.
   To stop the ship from sinking and to save each precious life,
   We threw all the cargo overboard including the captain's wife.

8. A farmer on his way to work he heard us loudly roar,
   And he threw us the ends of his gallusses and pulled us all ashore,
   I'm done with ocean ramblin' and roaming the ragin' main,
   And the next time I'll go to Lisburn, bejabbers I'll go by train.

The Lagan Canal

This song is similar in sentiment to 'The Cruise of the *Callabar*' and is the version favoured by James Hanna of Lisburn.

1. On the twentieth day of August, the day that we set sail,
   Bound for Molly Ward's with a cargo of India mail,
   Our ship's name, it was *Jane*, and the captain's name McFall.
   We were bound for foreign countries on the Lagan Canal.

2. When we came to Barbour's Quay, we saw a mighty man,
   His name was Kayley Shannon with a shovel in his hand.
   He said, 'Now boys, drop anchor, for I'm afraid your sails will fall,
   And there's goin' to be a ship-wreck on the Lagan Canal.'

3. The captain he came up on deck, a spy-glass in his hand,
   He said we were in great danger, for he couldn't see dry land,
   The mate he shouts, 'Put on more steam, for we are in distress,'
   When the engineer replied from the bank, 'The horse is doin' 'is best.'

4. The water it was very deep, it took us to the shins,
   We had a poor chance of our lives as none of us could swim.
   Then think of our wives and childer-en we might never see the more,
   When a postman threw us a bar of soap and we washed ourselves ashore.

5. They brought us all to Bridge Street, and got us all a bed,
   There wasn't one amongst us, but hadn't the staggers in the head,
   So now my song is ended, I hope it'll please you all,
   About that dreadful ship-wreck on the Lagan Canal.

Belfast Town

Both this and the following song refer to the Lagan, reminding us once more how its banks have for centuries been a favourite haunt of young lovers.

Belfast town now rich and great,
  Was then a village small,
And flocks of sheep grazed on that spot,
  Where stands the Linen Hall.

To herd the sheep was Mary's task,
  And she did not repine;
She looked so happy in her flock,
  She seemed almost divine.

And at that time young Dermott lived;
  The royal crown he wore;
He ruled the ground from Belfast town
  To Mourne's mountain shore.

To hunt the bear and savage wolf
  Was this young Prince's pride;
One day of age he killed three
  Beneath the Cave Hill side.

Returning from his weary chase,
  To give his horse some rest;
The reins upon his neck lay loose,
  To give his horse some breath.

And as he rode he Mary spied,
  Who rose in deep alarm:
She was sleeping on a primrose bank,
  With her cheek upon her arm.

And as she rose the Prince she knew,
  And quickly genuflexed;
She knew him by the golden star
  That glittered on his breast.

'O! maiden tell me who art thou,
  That dazzle so my eyes?
Are you a goddess from the skies,
  Or princess in disguise?'

'Oh, banter not a maiden fair,
  Of a low and mean degree.
My sovereign prince your pardon crave';
  With that she bent her knee.

'Trees on the Lagan' by William Conor

'For I am of a lowly birth,
  And Poverty beside.
My widowed mother lives with me,
  Upon the Lagan side.'

'Say that you are poor no more;
  Since those sweet charms of yours
Are far beyond in priceless wealth
  All gold or silver store.'

'Come with me and by my bride:
  Here is my heart and hand;
And I will share my throne with you
As Queen of Erin's land.'

Once more her snow white hand he pressed
  As they walked side by side,
Until they to the cottage came,
  Where her mother did reside.

'My worthy dame,' out spoke the Prince
  (The Prince of Mourne's land);
'The man has blessing on his youth
  That has thy daughter's hand.'

'My worthy prince,' replied the dame,
  'It's seventeen years and more
Since her I found outside my door,
  Half buried in the snow.

'And around her neck were jewels fine,
  And likewise gold in store,
To meet all charges till the time
  I might the child restore.'

And when the Prince the necklace saw,
  He started with delight,
Saying: 'Mary, dear, great is thy birth,
  And great's thy wealth and right.

'You are my uncle's long lost child,
  Which shall not be denied,
Since I have found at once this day
  A cousin and a bride.'

And when this royal pair was wed
  There rose with one loud roar
A general cheer from Belfast Lough
  To Mourne's Mountain Shore.

Mary of Sweet Belfast Town

One morning in July as early I strayed
By the banks of the Lagan I spied a young maid;
    Her cheeks were like roses
    And her hair was dark brown,
And her name it was Mary of Sweet Belfast Town.

I straightway walked to her and this did I say:
'Are you lovely Flora the goddess of May?
    Sure there's no beauty breathing
    Ah now, why would you frown?
Can vie with you Mary of Sweet Belfast Town.'

I said: 'Pretty fair maid, take pity, incline;
For my heart you have wounded, you angel divine:
    How gladly I'd ransom
    Some emperor's crown,
Just for to enjoy you in Sweet Belfast Town.'

And she answered and said: 'Please to mind what you're sayin',
For the young man I love has gone over the main;
    And I hear he is married on
    Some girl of renown,
Which is why I am single in Sweet Belfast Town.'

And it's when that he found she was loyal and true,
He said: 'Look, dearest Mary I've been true to you;
    For these seven long years
    I have roamed up and down,
But my heart was still with you in Sweet Belfast Town.'

She flew to his arms with much joy and surprise,
And she ate him alive with the love in her eyes;
    On a bank of primroses
    They both then sat down,
All near to the Lagan and Sweet Belfast Town.

And early next morning this couple they went
To the church to get married with every consent;
    And as he had great riches
    His love for to crown,
They live quite contented in Sweet Belfast Town.

Molly Bawn Lavery

This is a folk song of great lyric beauty. Again there are many variations in words and tune, adaptations often being made to suit the area where the song was being sung. The version quoted here was written by Pat Reynolds (a local poet) and comes from the Hume collection which was compiled at Beechfield in the townland of Ballykeel Artifinny, not two miles from the aqueduct where the scene of the drama is set. The song describes how James Reynolds went fowling by the Lagan late one evening and in the twilight mistook his sweetheart, Molly Bawn, for a swan and shot her dead. (In another version she was mistaken for a fawn, and in yet another a 'cran' (to rhyme with Bann).) James is said to have come home in a terrible state and pleaded with his father to help him leave the country for, he said, 'The Banns and the Bann Laverys, my life they'll swear away.'

It's all you young men that carry a gun
Beware of late fowling at the setting of the sun,
Concerning a young man that happened of late
That shot Molly Bawn Lavery, her beauty was great.

He being late fowling he shot her in the dark
But Oh and Alas he did not miss his mark,
With her apron about her he took her for a swan,
But Oh and Alas it was poor Molly Bawn.

But when he went to her and found she was dead
Abundance of tears from his eyes he has shed,
He went home to his Father with his gun in his hand,
Saying Father dear Father I have shot poor Molly Bawn.

It's outbespoke his Father, his hairs they were gray,
My son take my blessing and don't run away.
Stay in your own country, your trial to stand
And you will not be condemned by the laws of the land.

O Father dear Father I must go away
For in this country I never could stay
I shot Molly Bawn Lavery and she was my darling
The pride of the North and the Flower of Kilwarlin.

The maids of this country they are all very glad
Since Molly Bawn Lavery the beauty is dead.
But gather them together and put them all in a row
She appears in the middle like a mountain of snow.

She appeared to her Uncle as it were in a dream,
Saying Uncle dear Uncle James Reynolds don't blame
With my apron being about me he took me for a swan
But oh and alas it was I Molly Bawn.

In Lisburn she was born and in Lurgan educated
But oh in Kilwarlin poor Molly was defeated
With her apron being about her she was taken for a swan
But oh and alas it was poor Molly Bawn.

Bradley's lock (No. 21). From a watercolour
painted by Will Best (see Chapter V) in 1937.

Harry O'Rawe of 24 Lawrence Street, Belfast, worked as a hauler for five or six years after the First World War and must have often footed the twenty-seven miles of Lagan towpath. His poem 'The Lagan Canal' reminds us that though the canal ended at Lough Neagh, the boats continued across the Lough on the line of the tow towards other destinations. In this case the eventual destination, via the Ulster Canal, was Benburb.

The Lagan Canal
by Harry O'Rawe

Oh Molly Ward's, you're silent now,
Compared to days that have gone by,
When lighters lay there in a row,
To wait the day when they must go,
No engines then to drive them through,
Just line and horse and hauler too.
Through locks and bridges pretty slow,
For twenty-seven miles they go.
The men that sailed them were strong and tough,
Made of the good old Ulster stuff.
Their journey's end the Lagan through,
And Lough Neagh's shores are there in view.
A tug awaits them there at hand,
To cross the Lough into the Bann.
Nine miles up to Portadown,
With mills and factories all around.
Blackwater River runs on the fall,
With Coalisland another port of call
A nice wee town, lies on its own,
Set in the county of Tyrone.
The Moy comes next then Charlemont too,
The Ulster Canal is there in view.
So peaceful, still and undisturbed,
And further on is old Benburb.
Their load discharged, they turn around,
Back again for Belfast town.
Peat or sand they may collect,
Or a load of spuds tied up in sacks.
That journey o'er their work is done,
Ready they are for another run.
Those men have gone, the lighters too,
But the Lagan still remains in view.
Lorries have come and are here to stay,
God guide them safely on their way.

The verses which follow are taken from a longer poem by the late Thomas Reynolds of Ballyknock, Moira.

The Land I Love Best
by Thomas Reynolds

In pondering over the history of Trummery
  And wondering if more I should say,
It is with reluctance I leave it
  And once more I go on my way.
Where once stood Hertford's Bridge there are changes,
  For the old bridge no longer is there.
Missing too is the waterway
  And the barges that sailed it with care.

I remember as a boy from its towpath
  I fished in its waters so still;
Never once in those days did I think it
  A place in history would fill.
For a while let me pause and consider
  The new bridges that span the highway,
Where flowed the canal there is a roadway,
  These changes have taken place in my day.

The barges that were pulled by the horse
  Went past where I stand to Lough Neagh.
And many are the tales that could be told
  Of the place in history they played.
They say these changes were necesary
  To help progress on its way,
But the Lagan Canal and its history
  I must leave to some other day.

Oft by Beattie's Quay I had wandered
  In the past to pleasure my mind,
The architectural greatness of 'Equidock'
  You will search in vain for to find;
Why did they find cause to remove it,
  I find it hard for to say;
The Lagan Canal and its barges
  Are but memories of other days.
The journey with my thoughts it has ended
  The sun sinks low in the west.
Of all the lands I have seen and heard of,
  This is the one I love best.

'Snow on the Lagan' by William Conor

This poem came to me via Noel McMaster. The words were passed to him by a friend in Australia.

Where the River Lagan Flows

'Tis a lovely summer's evening in a dear old English park,
The thrush's notes are blending with the love song of the lark,
The children's merry voices are raised in happy glee
All mingling with the praises of the song bird's melody.
Yet spite of all the beauty and enchantment of the scene,
My thoughts are in old Ireland and her fields of verdant green,
And I think I see the honeysuckle winding round the rose
Near Lisburn, dear old Lisburn where the River Lagan flows.

I fancy I'm in Blaris on a fragrant summer morn,
I can hear the bees a-humming through the fields of yellow corn,
I can hear the landrail calling, to her timid little brood
While the blackbird sounds a warning from her shelter in the wood.
Then on through sweet Ravarnet I wander in a dream ,
I can see the fishes sporting in the silver tinted stream,
While Dromara's lofty mountain a purple shadow throws
O'er Lisburn, dear old Lisburn where the River Lagan flows.

The fertile plains of England have engaged the poet's pen,
And others sing the praises of the bonny Scottish glen,
But come with me to Ireland and see her beauties rare,
And visit Lisnagarvey and her fields and valleys fair.
There's not a spot on God's green earth such beauty can disclose
As Lisburn, dear old Lisburn where the River Lagan flows.

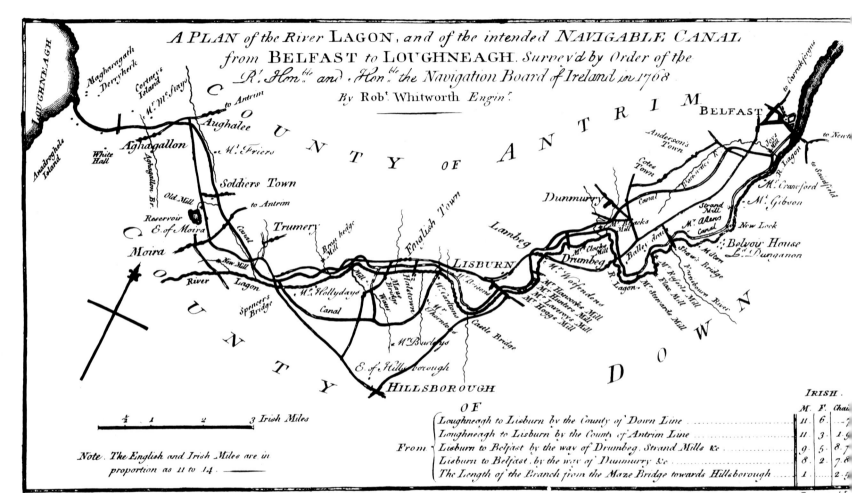

A PLAN of the River LAGON, and of the intended NAVIGABLE CANAL from BELFAST to LOUGHNEAGH. Survey'd by Order of the Rt. Honble. and Honble. the Navigation Board of Ireland in 1768. By Robt. Whitworth Enginr.

LOUGHNEAGH

COUNTY OF ANTRIM

COUNTY OF DOWN

BELFAST

to Carrickfergus

to North

to Southfield

Magharagath Derryherk
Cortney's Island
Mr. McStay
Aughalee
to Antrim
Mr. Friers
Aghagallon
White Hall
Soldiers Town
Old Mill
to Antrim
Reservoir E. of Moira
Aghagallon Br.
Moira
New Mill
Canal
River Lagon
Spencer's Bridge
Trumery
Bran hedge
Bran Mill
Mr. Hollydays
Canal
Mill
Maze Bridge
Halstowns
Mr. Carlands
Mr. Thornton
Mr. Burleys
E. of Hillsborough
HILLSBOROUGH
English Town
LISBURN
Mr. Thrisons
Castle Bridge
Lambeg
Mr. Woffendens
Mr. Hancocks Mill
Mr. Hunters Mill
Mr. Laverys Mill
Mr. Hoggs Mill
Drumbeg
Mr. Clockt Mill
R. Lagon
Mr. Stewards Mill
Dunmurry
Cotes Town
Canal
Anderson's Town
Blackwater R.
Mr. Bracks Mill
Strand Mill
Canal
Balley draft
Mr. Allens Canal
Shaws Bridge
Mr. Ryfords Mill
Flax Mill
Knockbourn River
Joys Mill
R. Lagon
Mr. Crawford
Mr. Gibson
New Lock
Belvoir House Lt. Dunganon
Mr. Allens
Mr. Milton

Amadroghels Island

¼ 1 2 3 Irish Miles

Note. The English and Irish Miles are in proportion as 11 to 14.

		IRISH.		
		M.	F.	Chai.
From	Loughneagh to Lisburn by the County of Down Line	11	6	7
	Loughneagh to Lisburn by the County of Antrim Line	11	3	1.9
	Lisburn to Belfast by the way of Drumbeg, Strand Mills &c	9	5	8.7
	Lisburn to Belfast by the way of Dunmurry &c	8	2	7.8
	The Length of the Branch from the Maze Bridge towards Hillsborough	1		2.5

OF

Bowen sculp.

VII

THE LAGAN
NAVIGATION

But where does a Northern Irelander find a canal to go walking beside, or boating upon? If he hasn't done so already, he will find the tow-paths of the old Lagan Navigation as pleasant a rambling place as any in the country.
Robert Hume, *Belfast Telegraph* 1971

The 'old Lagan Navigation', like several of Ulster's navigable waterways, came into existence in the eighteenth century, when Lough Neagh, the largest freshwater lake in the British Isles, became the hub of a network of canals serving a large area of Ulster. These included the eighteen-mile Newry Canal linking the town of Newry with the Upper Bann, Ducart's Canal which linked the once-promising Drumglass collieries with the Coalisland Canal, and the Coalisland Canal itself, which stretched for four and a half miles and entered the River Blackwater at the Canal-foot, three miles upstream from Lough Neagh. By the mid-nineteenth century the forty-six-mile Ulster Canal had also been opened taking the navigation through to Lough Erne, and improvements had been carried out on the Upper and Lower Bann. These consisted of dredging and deepening the river courses and the construction of locks, landing slips and quays at many points. Much of the traffic that passed along these waterways crossed Lough Neagh and entered the last waterway of the group, the Lagan Canal, at a point near Lurgan called Ellis' Gut.

It was an impressive network, but one largely doomed to failure, for Ulster's essentially rural community could not provide the volume of traffic required to support a commercial undertaking of this magnitude – a fact that the English and Dutch engineers who planned it had failed to realise. In addition, the original impetus for canal building in the province – the Tyrone coalfields – was itself impermanent. Ironically, coal was to become the main commodity carried inland in the opposite direction.

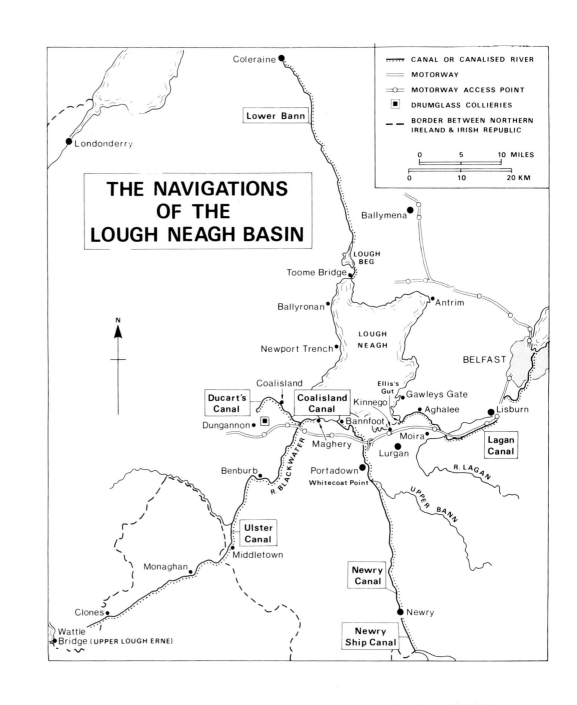

THE NAVIGATIONS
OF THE
LOUGH NEAGH BASIN

CANAL OR CANALISED RIVER
MOTORWAY
MOTORWAY ACCESS POINT
DRUMGLASS COLLIERIES
BORDER BETWEEN NORTHERN
IRELAND & IRISH REPUBLIC

0   5   10 MILES
0   10   20 KM

Coleraine

Lower Bann

Londonderry

Ballymena

LOUGH
BEG

Toome Bridge

Ballyronan

Antrim

LOUGH
NEAGH

Newport Trench

BELFAST

Coalisland

Ellis's
Gut

Gawleys Gate

Ducart's
Canal

Coalisland
Canal

Kinnego

Aghalee

Lisburn

Dungannon

Bannfoot

Maghery

Moira

Lagan
Canal

Lurgan

Benburb

Portadown

Whitecoat Point

R. LAGAN

UPPER BANN

Ulster
Canal

Middletown

Monaghan

Newry
Canal

Clones

Newry

Wattle
Bridge (UPPER LOUGH ERNE)

Newry
Ship Canal

The idea of linking Belfast with Lough Neagh was first mooted in the mid-seventeenth century, but it was not until a century later, encouraged by the success of the Newry Canal, that the thought was translated into action. In 1753, the Irish House of Commons passed an act for making the River Lagan navigable between Lough Neagh and the town of Belfast 'to increase the trade of Belfast and furnish the several inhabitants of the towns of Belfast, Lisburn, Moira and Hillsborough with many necessary materials of life in more plenty and at a cheaper rate than they can now be had'. The act set out that the inhabitants of these places were desirous and willing to be taxed in order that this could be accomplished. Thus it came about that on the 25th day of December 1753, and for eleven years after, there was levied an additional duty of excise of one penny a gallon on beer or ale, and fourpence a gallon on spirits to be raised from off the gauger's walk of Belfast, Lisburn etc. to provide the Commissioners of Inland Navigation with funds for building the new canal. (Strange that the votaries of alcohol should be made to pay for the privilege of water carriage!)

Construction on the Belfast-Lisburn section began in 1756 under Thomas Omer, an engineer of Dutch descent. Virtually no construction work was necessary on the first three miles – from the cross-channel quays as far as Stranmillis. In the early days loaded lighters approaching Stranmillis used a mast and sail assisted by a flowing tide and, if lucky, a following wind. Later, as on Lough Neagh, several lighters would be towed in a line behind a tug. Empty boats coming downstream were generally hauled as far as Stranmillis and then poled back to the quays.

Poling almost ceased after 1937 when the McConnell lock and tidal weir were brought into use about a mile downstream from Stranmillis.

Beyond Stranmillis the navigation ran partly in the River Lagan itself and partly, at places where the river made wide or awkward bends, in straight artificial channels called collateral cuts. In the two-and-a-quarter-mile length from Stranmillis to Shaw's Bridge, for instance, there were two stretches of river-cum-canal and three lengths of collateral cut. The work progressed favourably, and towards the end of 1756 the following item appeared in the *Belfast News Letter:*

> Alexander McClure in Belenoghan and Thomas Knox near Banbridge hath begun the canal near Drumbridge and want labourers. All good labourers may expect good usage and nine pence per day and their pay once a week.

'New' weir under construction at Lambeg. the foreground Dick Hanna, the weir-keepe poles himself along on a raft.

By 8 November 1757, the *News Letter* was able to report:

> The commissioners of the Lagan river navigation have so industriously applied the small fund arising from an additional duty of one penny a gallon on ale and four pence on spirits brewed and distilled in the towns of Belfast and Lisburn which in the best season does not amount to above £1,200 or £1,300 per annum and this last season next to nothing, but with that, and the small aid of £6,000 which they got out of the treasury last season, they have carried the navigation upwards of six miles from the town of Belfast; four locks are completed, four watch-houses, two

Lock, canal and Canal Street, Lisburn. On the extreme right is the lock-house designed by Richard Omer. Beside it is the house of the manager of the Island Mill.

navigation bridges, several miles of canal cut, the track road up to Drumbridge almost finished, the shoals mostly all dredged and removed and the fifth lock in great forwardness. Three pen-weirs for the use of the linen manufacture are also built, every one of them almost as expensive as a lock, and it is owned by the best judges who have seen these works that for strength and beauty they excel anything of the kind in the kingdom.

In addition to being responsible for the construction of the actual canal, the locks and bridges, Omer designed a number of the lock-houses, most of which are now in ruins. Omer's section of the canal was officially opened in 1763 and the *Belfast News-Letter* of 9 September that year describes the scene as follows:

On September 8, 1763, the *Lord Hertford*, a lighter capable of carrying 50 tons, made the first voyage on the new canal.

Mr. James Gregg, the owner, had invited a party to make the trip and to dine as his guests on board. Food of all descriptions was provided and 12 varieties of wine were served.

As the boat sailed along past bleach greens and fields where corn was being cut, a band aboard played popular airs. Hundreds of people stood on the banks of the river and walked along the towpath as far as Lisburn.

In Lisburn that evening the windows of many houses were

brightly illuminated and bonfires were blazing in the market place. Lord Hertford had instructed his agent to supply barrels of ale for those of the townspeople who wished to drink his health.

Dancing and merrymaking to the tunes of more than 50 fiddlers went on till the early hours of the morning.

There is little doubt that with the opening of the canal came great hopes for future prosperity in the area. Little did people realise that the system was to be beset by problems, some of them so serious that at times boats would not be able to sail.

By 1765, the river had been made navigable as far as Sprucefield, but then work ceased as the first problem, shortage of money, and the second problem, that of flooding in the river sections, had become apparent. There was also the problem of the vested interests of the linen bleachers who were sufficiently powerful to prevent the Commissioners of Navigation from having full control of the water supply.

In 1768 Omer's completed works were examined and strongly disapproved of by Robert Whitworth (assistant to the famous canal engineer James Brindley), mainly on the grounds that a river subject to floods would never in any circumstances make a satisfactory channel for navigation. Whitworth suggested that the only answer was to make a new channel, divorced entirely from the river, the most suitable course being on the northern side. Brindley approved of Whitworth's idea, but with finances in a precarious state there was no hope of the new plan being implemented. Nothing more was done, in fact, until 1779 when the then Earl (later first Marquess) of Donegall came to the rescue financially. In that year, the Company of Undertakers of the Lagan Navigation was set up, and by 1782, a new engineer, Richard Owen from Flixton in Lancashire began work on the Sprucefield – Lough Neagh section. Owen's first task involved the construction of a flight of locks to lift the level of navigation to its summit – a height of twenty-six feet above the level of the river at Sprucefield and one hundred and twelve feet above its level at Stranmillis. From Sprucefield the canal followed a course to the south of the river till just upstream from Spencer's Bridge where it crossed to the northern side by means of an aqueduct constructed from locally quarried sandstone. This eleven-mile summit level from Sprucefield to Aghalee was purely canal except for a short stretch which lay in the natural marshy valley of the Broadwater. To obtain a regular supply of water the navigators stemmed the waters of the Aghalee river which had previously flowed

*Wee poor Lightermen hopes your Lordship will excuse
my freedom in troubling you but it is our great distress
occasions it My Lord it is in regard of the Kinall for if
we lave Belfast an draws but 3 foot an half watter for
Lisborn, or this Place wee are generally detained at
least a fortnite or three weeks before wee can get home
My Lord the reason of that is for want of watter for the
Gentlemen that owens the Mils will not stop them for
to give us watter to help us up and the People that
owens the Locks takes no care of them for wee do not see
one of them from wee lave home untill wee go home again
but John Johnston an then it is to receive the lockage
My Lord wee pay let us have little or much 15
shilling of lockage to Lisburn and 16s and 3d to
Hillsborough My Lord between the dear lockage and
our long delay on the road has rendred us incapable of
keeping a house over our heads an our poor families is
almost lost by it an we have been tired speaking to John
Johnston to spake to the Commissioners an he says they
are angry at him when he spakes concerning it was it not
for that wee would not become troublesom but wee hope
that you will look upon us with an eye of pitty an
spake to the Gentlemen of the Board and occation the
Kenall to be cleaned for without your aid My Lord
there will be nothing done for us poor ditressed menn
My Lord wee hope you of your owen goodness will'
not neglect this an by so doing you will obtain a
blessing from God an our's shall shall bee foor your
Lordship fervently.*

Letter from lightermen to Lord
Hillsborough complaining about
shortage of water, *c.* 1790.

diagonally across it.

The final three and a half miles, with its series of ten locks descending to Lough Neagh, was completed by 1794. The completed canal was nearly twenty-seven miles in length and had twenty-seven locks. The maximum size of the boats it could accommodate was 62' x 14'6'' x 5'6''draft carrying 78 tons. It had cost £108,231, of which £43,304 had been provided by the government, £4,927 by the Lagan Navigation Company, and the remaining £60,000 by the Marquess of Donegall. The Marquess formally opened it by making the voyage from Richard Owen's house near Moira to Lough Neagh, where he was greeted by the firing of a cannon and the cheers of an assembled crowd.

During the next couple of decades the canal for some reason was allowed to fall into such disrepair that it was said that a ship could get to the West Indies and back in faster time than it took for a canal boat to do the round trip to Lough Neagh! A directive addressed to the Directors General of the Inland Navigation in 1811 stated:

. . . that the present communication by water between Belfast and Lough Neagh is defective in many respects in as much as the summit level is not sufficiently supplied with water during the summer, and the line which extends from Lisburn to Belfast, being partly in the bed of the river, is every winter rendered impassible by great and rapid floods which not only prevent the passage of lighters from the impetuosity of the current but generally overflow and sometimes carry away the banks, injure the locks and pen-weirs, and deposit such quantities of sand and gravel as create bars and shoals that cannot be removed until summer, thereby rendering the canal completely useless for at least one month of the year, and these obstructions usually take place at a time when the canal could be occupied most beneficially and usefully for the country in conveying flax seed to the interior [. . .] that the completion of these improvements would increase the trade and commerce of the towns of Belfast and Lisburn, the former of which contributes so very much to the revenue of this part of the United Kingdom, afford a cheap conveyance for coal from the Tyrone Collieries, improve the agriculture of the country by facilitating the export of grain and by enabling the proprietors of land adjacent to the canal and Lough Neagh to obtain an abundant supply of limestone at a

MONTHLY RETURN OF LIGHTERS – APRIL, 1858

(Sent in by John Brunton (Superintendent))

Date	Name	Cargo	Destination	Date	Name	Cargo	Destination
1	Speedwell	Coal	Lisburn	20	Thos. Maguire	Turf	Lake to summit
	Adelaide	Coal	Lisburn		Margaret	Coal	Lisburn
	Agnes	Wheat	Lake		Ann Jane	Wheat	Lisburn
3	Eliza	Coal	Head Level		Nemo	Sand	Lake to summit
	Thomas	Coal	Head Level	21	Maria	Coal	Head Level
	Dargan	Coal	Head Level		Frances	Coal	Lake
	William	Coal	Lisburn		Jane	Cinders	Lake
	Mary	Coal	Lisburn		Dargan	Coal	Head Level
	Dorothea	Coal	Lisburn		Margaret	Coal	Mossvale
	Jonathan	Coal	Lisburn		Mary	Coal	Head Level
	Mary	Coal	Head Level		Thomas	Coal	Lake
5	Nancy	Manure	Ballydrain		Hiskinson	Coal	Head Level
	William & John	Flour	Lisburn		Grace	Manure	Drumbridge
	Glenmoores	Coal	Lisburn	23	La Fayette	Coal	Lisburn
	Margaret	Coal	Mossvale		Thomas	Coal	Head Level
6	James & Ann	Coal	Lisburn		Dorothea	Coal	Head Level
	La Fayette	Coal	Lisburn	24	Eliza	Coal	Head Level
	Peggy	Coal	Head Level		Diligence	Coal	Lisburn
10	Martha	Coal	Head Level		Jonathan	Coal	Lambeg
	Ann Jane	Coal	Lisburn		Glenmoore	Wheat	Lake
	Huskinson	Coal	Lisburn		Mary Ann	Coal	Lisburn
12	Margaret	Coal	Mossvale		Margaret	Coal	Lambeg
	Cathern	Coal	Lake		Nancy	Coal	Lisburn
	Mary	Coal	Head Level	26	Frances & Isabella	Coal	Lisburn
	Eliza	Coal	Head Level		Ann Jane	Coal	Lisburn
	Packet	Cinders	Lake		Mary	Coal	Lisburn
	Mary Ann	Coal	Head Level		Grace	Manure	Drumbridge
	Jonathan	Coal	Lambeg		Perseverance	Tiles	from Lake
13	Jane	Tiles	from Lake		Nemo	Coal	Head Level
	Nancy	Tiles	from Lake		Speedwell	Coal	Lambeg
	Rory O'More	Flour	Lake to Lisburn		Susanna	Coal	Head Level
	James	Tiles	from Lake		Adelaide	Coal	Head Level
	Henry	Tiles	from Lake		Eliza	Coal	Head Level
13	Nancy	Manure	Ballydrain	28	La Fayette	Coal	Lisburn
14	Dorothea	Manure	Drumbridge		Jonathan	Coal	Lambeg
	Lupania	Coal	Head Level		Peggy	Coal	Head Level
	Adelaide	Coal	Head Level	29	Diligence	Indian Corn & flour	Lisburn
15	Diligence	Wheat	from Head Level				
16	Margaret	Coal	Lambeg		Burton	Turf	from Lake to Summit
17	Speedwell	Coal	Lisburn		John & William	Sand	Belfast
	Jonathan	Coal	Mossvale		Nancy	Coal	Lambeg
	Peggy	Coal	Head Level		Margaret	Coal	Lambeg
19	Mary Ann	Coal	Head Level		Mary Ann	Coal	Lisburn
	Frances & Isabella	Coal	Lisburn		Maria	Salt & Coal	Head Level
	1 Raft		Lisburn				
	Mary	Coal	Lisburn	30	Grace	Sand	Drumbridge
	William	Coal	Lisburn		Frances & Isabella	Sand	Lisburn
					Dorothea	Manure	Drumbridge

moderate expense and would materially tend to encourage the manufacturers and promote the convenience and prosperity of a large portion of the most populous of the province of Ulster.

The canal had by this stage been taken over by a group of local businessmen who decided to repair and modernise it. After this, trade improved considerably and in 1825 the Secretary of the Navigation wrote:

Last year 546 lighters passed up and down, the average burthen of which was about 45 tons or in all 26,000. I do not think the trade on the Newry Canal was equal tho' it did most in grain. Had not the last summer been usually dry and the winter unusually wet I am convinced our trade would have been one-fourth more. I am quite convinced that the statement made of the expected trade on the Ulster Canal will be realized.

And by 1838 the Ordnance Survey Memoirs for the parish of Blaris stated:

. . .nine hundred lighters have passed up and down the canal loaded averaging 50 tons each from 5 January 1836 to 5 January 1837, also timber which is generally brought up in rafts. These crossing Lough Neagh are towed after a lighter.

It is worth recording that similar memoirs for the parish of Aghagallon stated at the same time:

This canal was cut at enormous expense to judge from the replies of people on its banks. They say it cost as many guineas as would extend from Belfast to the lough supposing them to be laid in a row touching each other. Vessels of from 25 to 30 tons trade up the canal. The charge is five shillings per ton for potatoes and they also bring timber from Belfast to Tyrone and Armagh coasts, also slates, iron, sugar, coals and tar, in fact anything that will go into their boats they have no objection to. The dues paid by the boats at the locks are 5d. for the opening of each flood gate or £2.10s.0d. for the whole voyage.

QUAYS 11.6.29
(STRANMILLIS – LOUGH NEAGH)

Name and Distance from 1st Lock		Owners	Remarks
¹/₈ ml.		L.N. Co.	Generally potatoes discharged.
–	Newforge	–	No longer used.
4 ml.	Edenderry	John Shaw Brown	Coal discharged for factory.
5½ ml.	Drumbridge	L.N. Co.	Coal and sand discharged.
–		–	–
6¼ ml.	Mossvale	Charley, Seymour Hill.	Coal discharged.
6⁷/₈ ml.	Chrome Hill	Lambeg Wvg Co.	Coal discharged.
7¼ ml.	Lambeg	Lambeg Bleaching Co.	Coal discharged.
7¾ ml.	Glenmore	Glenmore	Coal discharged.
8¹/₁₆ ml.	Hilden	Wm. Barbour & Sons	Coal discharged.
8⁵/₈ ml.	Millbrook	Glenmore	Coal discharged.
9 ml.	No. 12 lock	Island Spinning Co.	Coal discharged.
9¹/₈ ml.	Public Quay, Lisburn	L.N. Co.	General discharge.
9¹/₈ ml.	Millar & Stevenson	Millar & Stevenson	Coal discharged.
9¼ ml.	Lagan	Lagan Factory	Coal discharged.
9½ ml.	Pedlows	Pedlow's Factory	Coal discharged.
11 ml.	Blaris Quay & Union Locks	L.N. Co.	Coal discharged.
12⁵/₈ ml.	Newport	L.N. Co.	Hillsborough Factory
12⁵/₈ ml.	Newport	East Downshire Co.	Coal discharged.
13½ ml.	Kesh	Mr. Paul McHenry	Coal discharged.
17 ml.	Nocher's Quay	L.N. Co.	Coal discharged.
18¼ ml.	Boyle's Bridge	Mr. Agnew	Coal discharged.
19 ml.	Lady Bridge	L.N. Co.	Coal discharged.
20 ml.	Soldierstown	L.N. Co.	In ruins
22 ml.	Aghalee	L.N. Co.	Coal discharged.
22¾ ml.	Lurgan Rd, Aghalee	L.N. Co.	Potatoes loaded.
23½ ml.	Goudy Bridge	L.N. Co.	Potatoes loaded.
25 ml.	Cranagh Bridge	L.N. Co.	Potatoes loaded.
26¼ ml.	Ellis' Gut	L.N. Co.	Potatoes loaded.

L.N. Co. = Lagan Navigation Company.

Kinnego Harbour (Port Lurgan). Although Ellis's Gut marked the end of the Lagan Canal, it was not the final destination of canal traffic. Lighters proceeded across Lough Neagh to Coalisland, Newry, Portglenone and other destinations. The nearest was this one at Kinnego. To the left can be seen barges discharging coal for Andrew Murray and W.J. Green & Co.

In 1843, the property was vested in the Lagan Navigation Company and the time for the return trip was reduced to one week. The company prospered until it accepted responsibility for the Ulster and Coalisland canals in 1888. These had never paid their way and now became a heavy drain on the resources of the Lagan route. In spite of this the Lagan company made a profit for many years, carrying at its height 174,000 tons of cargo annually. After 1910, trade gradually decreased, dropping to 46,000 tons in 1938. There was a slight revival during the War when barges were taken over by the army but after the war little traffic offered and the company's income dwindled while expenditure increased. In spite of having received financial aid from the government over a period of years the end was not far away. In 1954 the Lagan Navigation Company was officially dissolved and its property as described below was handed over to the Ministry of Commerce.

All the estate right title and interest of the Company to and in the property acquired by it under and by virtue of The Lagan Navigation Acts 1843–88 or otherwise howsoever and wheresoever situate including all lands tenements and hereditaments and all waters, watercourses, bridges, sluices, drains, locks, weirs, banks, dams, roads, towing paths and other ways rights privileges and advantages whatsoever and all barges boats effects utensils and materials used in connection with the undertaking and all tolls or funds claims titles and possessions of what nature or kind so ever situate in Northern Ireland.

All easements; quasi-easements; accommodations and all rights owned used or enjoyed by the Company for the purposes of or in connection with the Undertaking over across or on any lands other than those herein mentioned.

It was the end of the road, not only for the Lagan but virtually all Ulster's inland navigations. No one would dispute the fact that as a commercial enterprise the day of the canal is over. The reason for its demise is not hard to understand. It could not compete with modern transport either in speed or cost and that bane of all canal builders, shortage of water on the summit, was a 'running sore' throughout its century and a half of useful life. Yet it is a tribute to the ease of water transport that two men, a horse and a barge with five and a half feet of water underneath could transport eighty tons of merchandise any distance albeit only at walking pace.

A well-known crew approaches Drumbridge
– Attie and Jane Mullen on board the
Shamrock. The hauler is Johnny Douglas. At
this point the horse sometimes walked in the
water to 'line the boat up' for going under the
bridge.

EPILOGUE

Where barges once plied their leisurely way 'up country', now runs a modern roadway, for most of the eleven-mile summit level was filled in during the construction of the Sprucefield–Moira section of the Dungannon motorway. It is a far cry from the days when a lighterman could wait for days, even weeks, before discharging his boat-load of coal; in one instance a boat lay out for three weeks – so that a wild duck could bring out her young.

As the traffic rushes along the motorway to-day through this 'same' pleasant countryside, it is difficult to visualise the horse plodding along the tow-path with its heavy load past places like the Reedmakers, Twigger's Corner, and Barney's Basin. Long after more recent things are forgotten, there will surely be a place in history for the canal and the canal folk; people like Joe McVeigh, 'Hell's Fire' Jack McCann, Hughie Bann and the dozens of other characters who brought life and activity to the Lagan for nearly two hundred years.

A bonus not shared by all canals was the all-pervading loveliness of a Lagan Valley then unmarred by the pollution, litter and squalor that are the trademarks of our civilization. A trip along its quiet waters in those far-off days must surely have rested both the eyes and the soul. Yet the fact that the area has now been designated a regional park is a reminder that much of it is still beautiful. In the words of an anonymous poet:

> No need to search afar
> To wander wide
> Seeking some ultimate star;
> E'en where the many are,
> She doth abide.
> Beauty is close at hand.
> Daily you breathe her breath.
> Her feet your ways have trod
> Yea! near as Life and Death
> As near as God.

SOME CANAL TERMS

A Barge Horn

A Breaker

aqueduct   bridge carrying water or a canal across a valley or river

bank-ranger   person employed to maintain the canal banks

barge horn   horn used to warn of an approaching lighter

basin *or* **bight**   wider part of canal where one boat could pull in to allow another to pass

breaker   small keg or barrel for drinking water

cut or gut   narrow channel of water

dock, dry   basin-like structure which can be emptied of water to allow repairs to be made to the bottom of a boat

dock, puddle   place where clay was dug out and mixed with water to make a watertight lining for the canal

draught   the depth of a loaded boat or lighter in the water

gauger   collector of excise duty, especially on liquor

gunwale   upper edge of the side of a boat or lighter

hauler   man who walked with the lighter horse

ice-boat   iron boat used for breaking ice

larboard   the left side of a boat when facing the bow

level   stretch of water between two locks

  head level *or* **summit level**   highest level

light   (of boat) unladen

lighter   flat-bottomed boat, barge

lock   part of canal cut off to form separate basin between two levels

monkey-box   drawer for metal polish and cleaning-gear

Pen-weir, bridge and overfall at Lisburn. The apparatus for raising or lowering the gate of the weir can be seen in the centre of the bridge.

Hauler's single-tree. The barge rope was attached to the centre hook, the traces to the outer two.

quarters   bows of a boat or lighter

pen-weir   kind of dam across river. Water builds up behind the weir to the required depth, then flows over the top

pole   put shoulder to barge pole and push against something to move a boat in the water

sam(p)son   strong post on boat to which tow-rope was attached

scow   flat-bottomed boat used for repair work

scuttle   hatchway

shear-legs *or* **sheer-legs**   poles attached at or near top, tripod fashion; used for discharging cargo

shoal *or* **showl**   submerged bank of mud, sand or gravel

single-tree   wooden part of horse's harness to which the tow-rope was attached

sluice   the body of water controlled by a sluice-gate

sole   floor (of lighter cabin)

stop-gates   wooden gates used to separate one stretch of water from another which was to be drained for repairs; used where there were no lock-gates, e.g. on the summit level

stour   dust

toll-tickets   official dockets issued by the Navigation Company stating details of cargo, destination, etc.

towpath   path beside a river or canal used by people or horses hauling boats

traces   chains connecting part of a horse's harness to the single-tree

troll   to fish with dead-bait or spoon-bait trailed in water, often behind boat

wheep   whistle

whopped   (of hay) thrashed and gathered into bundle

No. 9 lock, looking towards Lisburn. The
premises of Lambeg Bleaching Dying and
Finishing Co. Limited were behind the wall
on the left.

LOCKS

No.	Name by which known	Situation
1.	Molly Ward's	Stranmillis
2.	Mickey Taylor's	Moreland's Meadow
3.	McLeave's	Newforge
4.	Rosie's	Edenderry
5.	Ballydrain	Ballydrain
6.	The Drum	Drumbeg
7.	McQuiston's	Mossvale
8.	The High Bridge	Ballyskeagh
9.	Lambeg	Lambeg
10.	Hilden	Hilden
11.	Scott's	Hilden
12.	Lisburn	Lisburn
13.	Becky Hogg's	Lisburn
14–17.	The Union Locks	Sprucefield
18.	Aghalee	
19.	Wood Lock (Dan Horner's)	Aghalee
20.	Sheerin's	Area
21.	Bradley's	
22.	Cairn Lock	
23.	Prospect Lock	Aghagallon
24.	Goudy Lock	Area
25.	Fegan's (Turtle Dove Lock)	
26.	Cranagh (Chapel Lock)	
27.	Ellis' Gut	Lough Neagh

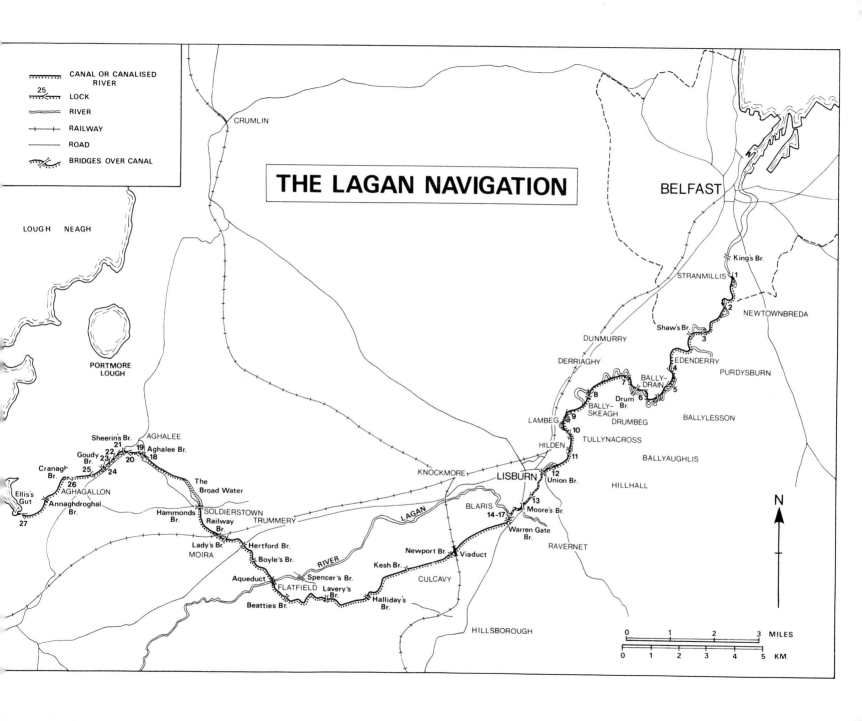

THE LAGAN NAVIGATION

CANAL OR CANALISED RIVER
25 LOCK
RIVER
RAILWAY
ROAD
BRIDGES OVER CANAL

BELFAST

LOUGH NEAGH

PORTMORE LOUGH

CRUMLIN

King's Br.

STRANMILLIS 1

2

NEWTOWNBREDA

Shaw's Br.

3

DUNMURRY

EDENDERRY

DERRIAGHY

4

PURDYSBURN

BALLY-DRAIN

7

5

Drum Br. 6

8

BALLY-SKEAGH

DRUMBEG

BALLYLESSON

LAMBEG

9

10

HILDEN

TULLYNACROSS

Sheerin's Br. AGHALEE

21

19 Aghalee Br.

Goudy 22

Br. 23 20 18

25 24

11

BALLYAUGHLIS

Cranagh Br.

26

KNOCKMORE

LISBURN

12 Union Br.

HILLHALL

AGHAGALLON

The Broad Water

Ellis's Gut

27

Annaghdroghal Br.

Hammonds Br. SOLDIERSTOWN

Railway Br.

TRUMMERY

LAGAN

BLARIS

13

Moore's Br.

14-17

Warren Gate Br.

RAVERNET

Lady's Br. MOIRA

Hertford Br.

Boyle's Br.

RIVER

Newport Br. Viaduct

Aqueduct

Spencer's Br.

FLATFIELD Lavery's Br.

Kesh Br.

CULCAVY

Beatties Br.

Halliday's Br.

HILLSBOROUGH

N

0   1   2   3 MILES

0 1 2 3 4 5 KM.

POSTSCRIPT

It is strange and wonderful to see at last the first copies of the book you have spent so long researching and writing. After the initial enthusiasm wears off however, you take a longer, more critical look and then you begin to see the things that might have improved it, the things you should have added, the things you should have left out, and you notice also those errors that somehow, despite all that checking, have crept into the text. The prospect of a reprint provides therefore a welcome opportunity to correct a few infelicities.

Readers who have seen the map of the Lagan *circa* 1876 in the Belfast Boat Club's pamphlet, *The First 100 Years*, will be aware that Molly Ward's tavern did not occupy the same site as Molly Ward's lock-house, as is implied on p.5, but was in fact some distance to the south, on the opposite side of the water. The Kilpatrick family tree shows that Mary Kilpatrick married one James McCann, not Edward Hogg, as stated on p.30. The document referred to on p.35 was omitted by mistake and is reproduced opposite.

Apologies to Cyril Healey for inadvertently referring to him as Cyril Heaney throughout Chapter III, and to Lord Tennyson for wrongly attributing the lines from 'The Lady of Shalott' quoted on p.50 to Rudyard Kipling. Apologies are also due to Dr W.A. McCutcheon for leaving out the caption to the splendid photograph of barges at the Queen's Bridge (p.122) which he allowed us to reproduce from his collection. The people on the lower deck in the photograph on p.82 are in fact Michael Kidd and James Hanna, while in the foreground are the men from the Ministry, Messrs Foster and Montgomery. The Omer lock-house is on the extreme *left* of the picture on p.113 and the manager's house is opposite it, on the other side of the canal. In the photograph on p.119 the barges discharging coal are in the far distance to the right, not the left. An unfortunate misprint on p.58 has Coolie Dan Mulholland sending Harry McCourt off to the bed of the mysterious red-head; what he actually said was, of course, 'Away back to *yer* bed'! And it was Bob Stewart, not Bob Dugan, who offered hospitality to the thirsty at the Drum (see p.52). The engineer's report mentioned on p.77 has not in fact been reproduced.

There were many other avenues of research which for various reasons were not explored in this book – which is hardly surprising, since the Lagan has been a source of inspiration for writers and artists for centuries. I can only hope that my book will lead others to take up where I have left off and investigate an area of local history that I have found both fascinating and rewarding.

May Blair, November 1981

SHIPPED in good Order and well Conditioned, by Ralph Bullock in and upon The good Ship Called the 'Charles' John Murray whereof is Master for this present Voyage, and now riding at Anchor in the Quay at Soldierstown, and bound for Antrim forty Tuns of wheat in Bulk being Marked and Numbered as in the Margin, and are to be delivered in the like good Order, and well conditioned at the aforesaid Port of Antrim (All Dangers, Damages, Losses or Accidents on the Seas, of what kind soever, Fire, and Piratical Robberies, excepted) unto order or to his Assigns, he or they paying for the said goods, FREIGHT Six Shillings per Tun with Primage and Average accustomed. In witness thereof the master or Purser of the said Ship hath affirmed to three Bills of Lading, all of this Tenor and Date; one of which Bills being accomplished, the other two to stand void. Dated in Soldierstown 13th January 1813.